Resources for Junior Highs in the Church

Volume 3

Barbara Middleton,
Editor

Judson Press® Valley Forge

EXPLORE, VOLUME 3

Copyright © 1978
Judson Press, Valley Forge, PA 19481

Unless otherwise indicated, Bible quotations in this volume are in accordance with the Revised Standard Version of the Bible, copyrighted 1946, 1952, 1971, 1973 © by the Division of Christian Education of the National Council of the Churches of Christ in the United States of America, and are used by permission.

Also quoted in this book:

The Holy Bible, King James Version.

Library of Congress Cataloging in Publication Data
Main entry under title:

Explore; resources for junior highs in the Church.

  Vol. 2 edited by J. E. Grant; vol. 3 edited by B. Middleton.
  Includes bibliographies.
  1. Church work with adolescents. 2. Christian education of adolescents. 3. Youth—Religious life.
I. Corbett, Janice M. II. Grant, James E.
III. Middleton, Barbara.
BV1475.9.E88   268'.433   74-8574
ISBN 0-8170-0646-X

Using EXPLORE, VOLUME 3

Explore, Volume 3, is a RESOURCE book.
This means:

- You don't have to use everything in the book.
- You don't have to follow the order of the book.
- You can pick and choose, change and adapt.
- You can make the book *work for you,* rather than make yourself *work for the book.*

Explore, Volume 3, IS A TOOL FOR JUNIOR HIGH MINISTRY. Pick it up . . . get the "feel" of it . . . use it to mold a ministry that has meaning for YOUR GROUP.

To use *Explore, Volume 3,* follow these steps:

1. First look through *Explore, Volume 3,* and discover the many program resources, the additional program ideas, the helps for you as leader, and the additional resource suggestions.

2. Then, take *Explore, Volume 3,* to your next planning meeting with junior highs. *After* you have determined the current needs and interests of the group *and* decided on the goals for the upcoming group times, look to see if any of the program ideas in *Explore, Volume 3,* will help you in reaching those goals.

3. When you decide to use a program, be sure to read through the entire plan. Check each suggested activity, and ask if it will work for you. Are there other activities which might be better to try?

4. Check on the time each activity needs, and compare the total time required with the time you have available. Do you need to eliminate some activities or add some more from the suggestions in the "Additional Program Ideas" section?

5. Write out your step-by-step plan. Make sure you include some recreational time, some warm-up activities, the major content activities, and a closing experience for the entire group.

6. Do the necessary preparation and gather the materials you will need.

7. TRY IT. Then, when finished, EVALUATE IT. Decide what went wrong and right. Use your experience to plan a better experience next time.

8. Having a special problem? Read the appropriate article in LEADERSHIP HELPS.

9. Want to find some more resources to add to *Explore, Volume 3?* Thumb through the pages of ADDITIONAL RESOURCES. Also, look through the INDEX since there may be a program resource in an earlier volume you may wish to use.

A SPECIAL THANKS

Explore, Volume 3, has been written by many people who work with junior highs in churches. Their names are included with each program or article. Special thanks to them and to the planning committees who helped shape this volume: Eva Emmons, Robert Hinkley, Miriam Eckard, Barbara Middleton, and the junior high group of Plymouth Valley Baptist Church, Norristown, Pennsylvania.

CONTENTS

ADDITIONAL PROGRAM IDEAS

LEADERSHIP HELPS

FAITH
FAITH
FAITH

FAITH

FAITH

I am what I am—God

KNOWING GOD   Franklin W. Nelson

GOALS

To help youth to express their thoughts about God, to share their feelings about God's authority, and to become aware of God's caring presence in their lives.

WHY?

Junior high young people have reached an age of advanced thinking. They are able to think about the deeper meanings behind words and symbols. Many church young people have moved through years of Sunday church school and may be saying to themselves, "Hey, wait a minute! Some of the stuff that they taught me is in the Bible doesn't make a lot of sense to me anymore. Is there a God? And if there is, does God really care about the kinds of struggles I'm going through right now?"

The most important symbol in our faith is the word "God." Junior highs need opportunities to express their thoughts about God. They need to "own" (admit and accept) their own thoughts and be able to say, "This is what I really think, whether or not I am supposed to think it." So it is important that they examine their thoughts and feelings.

The concepts of God that our churches teach sometimes communicate the judging, authoritative attributes of our Creator even more than the loving, listening, accepting characteristics. Junior highs have a tendency, even if in subtle ways, to reject persons in authority over them (parents, teachers, police); the tendency is also there to reject the authority of God in their lives. Junior highs need to learn to trust the loving authority of God far more than the condemning authority.

PREPARATION

Materials needed: newsprint or chalkboard
felt-tipped pens or chalk
typing paper
crayons and pens
masking tape
Bibles
string and ring (for game)
record or cassette music

Warning   Beware of using this resource book in front of your youth. Prepare yourself in a way that all important notes and activities are on another sheet of paper or in a notebook. Why? Youth want *you*, not a book, to lead the program. You are the most important resource.

PROCEDURE

Step 1: Recreation (10 minutes)

Begin with an active game which involves the whole group. You may want to try "Ring on a String." Here's how it's done: Form a circle by holding hands. Drop hands and then stretch a string around the inside of the circle. Have everyone hold their hands palms down on the string. Before tying the knot, put a ring on a string. The person who is "It" stands in the middle of the circle, as the players pass the ring from person to person, and tries to discover who has the ring. The person caught with the ring is "It."

Step 2: Drawings (20 minutes)

Explain that you would like each youth to give some thought to his or her idea of God. "Who is God to you? What is God like? How have you seen or known God in the past few weeks?" Give them a minute to relax, close their eyes, and think about this question.

Next, say something like this: "We all have our own personal ideas or images of God. We are all different, and so we think of God in different ways. To get us going, I'd like to ask you each to express your idea of God by drawing a picture of God. This can be a symbol or a picture that you feel represents God. There are no good or bad, right or wrong pictures. We're not all artists, either. That's OK. Just give some thought to your idea of God, and then begin to draw. There are materials on the table for you; so go ahead. You'll have only about ten minutes to work on it; so don't try to do a masterpiece."

After they have started their pictures and it appears that most of them are working, interrupt them and say, "I'd like to have you put these words at the bottom of your picture: 'GOD IS LIKE. . . .' (Note: The leader should put these words at the top of a piece of newsprint.) Complete the sentence, 'God is like. . . .' When you are finished, take a piece of masking tape and display your drawing on the wall. Add your 'God is like' statement to the list on the newsprint. Go ahead and browse when you're finished."

There may be some resistance at first to drawing a picture. However, junior highs can do a very good job of expressing themselves in this way. If someone is having a very difficult time, talk to him or her individually and suggest that if he or she would rather write a poem or make a brief statement about God, that would be OK.

It might help also to set a mood for creativity by playing a record or cassette of orchestral music, such as *Jonathan Livingston Seagull* or some other instrumental music.

Step 3: God Is Like . . . (5 minutes)

After the group has finished browsing, bring the group together and read the "God is like" statements out loud. Take some time to add to the list other thoughts that come to their minds, such as "God is like the wind that blows in the trees." "God is like finding the ring on a string."

Take some time for a little discussion and then make some summarizing comments, such as "The way we think about God either makes God very real to us or very unreal. God must be more than someone in the clouds somewhere. Until we realize that God is a part of our lives and cares about us and wants the best for us, our God is too small. Our ideas of God change from year to year, and that's good, because we are all maturing in our knowledge of God."

Step 4: Continua (15 minutes)

Prepare newsprint with the following on it in large print:

When I do something I know is wrong or when I fail, *God* makes me feel:

Guilty _____	OK
Judged _____	Forgiven
Like quitting _____	Like trying again
Rejected _____	Accepted

Have each person get another piece of paper and copy these continua, putting an *X* where it best describes his or her feelings. Have each person work alone.

As soon as they are finished, have the young people transfer their *X*s to the newsprint. Be careful to give this instruction when they are almost done. The purpose is to share what everyone feels. Summarize briefly.

WHY?

The purpose of this exercise is to allow youth to express their feelings about God's authority. The leader might ask, "Do these youth see God primarily as a condemning or loving God? As negative and oppressive, or positive and helpful?"

In all of these exercises keep an eye open for the religious thinking of various individuals. Since we are all at different stages in our religious development, you might try to discover special areas where more growth is needed in your youth's concepts of God.

Step 5: Scripture (5 minutes)

Read 1 John 2:3-6 and ask this question: "According to this Scripture, how does one come to know God? Do you think it is all of a sudden? Gradual? Or both?" Discuss this Scripture with the group.

Step 6: Closing (10 minutes)

Form a circle (either sitting or standing) and then read Exodus 3:13-15. Explain that the Hebrew name for God translates "I am," or literally "I am what I am." Suggest to them that we can never define God completely or truly know God with our human intelligence. However, there are many ways in which

God is revealed to us. Have each person think of one way in which he or she has seen God or come to know God better, and then have each one say, "I met God . . ." and finish the statement. The whole group should then respond in unison after each statement, "I am what I am." Go around the circle so that each person can make a statement. Close with prayer.

ADDITIONAL PROGRAM IDEAS

—After Step 1 choose a song(s) that speaks about God, and have a time of singing (10 minutes).

—After Step 2 take time to share and discuss the drawings in pairs or groups of three. This may open up many topics of interest and concern that might be considered as program ideas for the future (5-10 minutes).

—After Step 2 have the youth cut out of magazines pictures that in some way show God. Share some of the pictures with the group. Fill a bulletin board with the pictures (15-20 minutes).

—After Step 3 write a song or poem using the "God is like" statements (10 minutes).

—During Step 4 you might try human continua. Have the length of the room be the line, and have each person stand on the line about where his or her *X* was. Choose only one or two of the continua for this.

—After Step 4 try this exercise: On newsprint, write "I am to God as . . .

a puppet is to a _____."
a building is to a _____."
a painting is to a _____."
a window is to a _____."
a bicycle is to a _____."
an *a* is to a _____."

Have each person write his or her response on paper and then discuss the responses in groups of two or three (10 minutes).

—Begin a topical Bible study on God and God's characteristics. If the interest is high, a Bible study could be very exciting and interesting for future programs.

—Role-play situations at school, home, church, or wherever God is seen as real. Discuss these.

—Create banners using the "God is like" statements.

Franklin W. Nelson is pastor of the First Baptist Church in Knoxville, Iowa. He has also been the associate pastor of the First Baptist Church, Davenport, Iowa, with special responsibilities for Christian education and youth ministries.

FAITH

how do you relate to someone who lived 2000 years ago?

EXPERIENCING A RELATIONSHIP WITH JESUS CHRIST Franklin W. Nelson

GOAL

To help youth experience a seeing, trusting, hearing relationship with one other person in the group in order to understand better what a knowing, believing, listening relationship is with Jesus Christ.

WHY?

One of the most important aspects of Christianity is that we come to God through our knowledge and relationship with Jesus Christ. And yet, how does that happen for the junior high youth in terms she or he can understand? How does a junior high relate to someone who lived two thousand years ago when his or her concerns are primarily about "today" relationships?

It is through our relationships with parents, friends, peers, and others that we are able to begin to understand what relationship with Jesus Christ means. Many junior highs have made a basic commitment of belief in and acceptance of Christ and are trying to improve their relationships with Christ. Others have not committed themselves to Christ and yet may be interested. All of us could improve our relationships. At whatever point in our spiritual pilgrimage we now are, we need a deeper understanding of how to relate to this Someone who lived two thousand years ago.

PREPARATION

Materials needed: newsprint or chalkboard
masking tape
felt-tipped pens or chalk
blindfold for each (optional)
Bible for each person
music on record or cassette
pencils
chairs (see Step 2, Experience 2)

Using some newsprint, display the title "How Do You Relate to Someone Who Lived 2000 Years Ago?" on the wall. Prepare the other pieces of newsprint ahead of time (see Steps 2 and 3).

Beware of holding this book in your hand when your are leading this program. Know beforehand what you are going to do and write it down on a separate sheet of paper or in a notebook.

PROCEDURE

Step 1 (5-10 minutes)

Have your regular opening and greeting. Take care of any announcements at this time. Sing a song or play a quick group game that is a favorite.

Step 2: Relational Experiences (20 minutes)

Put on newsprint (or chalkboard) in big letters the words "RELATIONSHIP DEPENDS ON. . . ."

11

Divide the group into pairs. Do this in such a way that the group will be mixed and each person will not be talking to his or her usual friends. For example, number off; or hand each person a colored ticket when he or she arrives, and have each get with someone who has the same colored ticket.

Now introduce the next three experiences by saying something like, "Let's spend some time experiencing a relationship with one other person."

Experience 1

Have each of the partners look carefully at the other and examine him or her closely. The purpose of this is to see as much as possible about that person physically so that when there is a change, one can detect it. Now have one of the partners turn around while the other makes a change in his or her physical appearance (such as changing a watch, ring, buttons, or whatever). Now have the partner turn face to face again to see if he or she can see the change. Reverse the roles and let the second partner test the first.

Allow for some laughter and good-natured sharing and then conclude, "One of the things that a relationship depends on is SEEING—KNOWING." (Put these words on the newsprint under "RELATIONSHIP DEPENDS ON. . . .")

Experience 2

Keep the same partners and provide one chair for each pair. Spread out around the room. Blindfold one of the partners (or have them close their eyes). Now tell them that their partner will be putting a chair behind their knees. They are to fold their arms in front of them and, without feeling for the chair, sit down. Reverse the roles.

Ask, "Did you trust, or believe, that the other person put the chair in place?"

Conclude, "Another one of the things that relationships depend on is TRUST—BELIEVING." (Add these words to the list on the newsprint under "SEEING—KNOWING.")

Experience 3

Have the same partners sit on the floor, or in chairs, facing each other and in some way touching. Have written on another sheet of newsprint the following questions for one-to-one conversations:

What would you like in a friend?

Tell about a gift you have received and why it was special to you.

If you could give anything in this world to your best friend, what would it be?

Have the partners share one or all of these questions with each other, but stress to them the importance of really hearing what the other actually means (not just the words, but the feelings behind the words).

After five to ten minutes conclude: "Relationship also depends on hearing another person." (Write "HEARING—LISTENING—SHARING" under "TRUSTING—BELIEVING.")

Step 3: Scripture Study (15 minutes)

Bring the whole group close together in a circle on the floor or in chairs near the newsprint. To begin this Scripture study, introduce it by saying something like, "Our relationship to our Lord and friend Jesus Christ is a lot like our relationships to each other. Our relationship to Jesus Christ also depends on *seeing* and *knowing* Christ." (Circle these words on the newsprint.) "How well do we really *know* Jesus? And what does that mean?

"Our relationship to Jesus Christ also depends on *trusting* and *believing* in Christ for who Christ was and is." (Circle these words.) "How well do we trust and believe in Jesus Christ?

"And our relationship to Jesus Christ depends on *hearing* and *listening* to Christ as well as *sharing* our life with Christ." (Circle these words.)

Divide the larger group into three smaller groups; and give Group 1 note card 1, Group 2 note card 2, and Group 3 note card 3, as follows:

Card 1	SEEING—KNOWING John 1:10-14; 1 John 1:1-4 What do these Scriptures tell us about a relationship to Jesus Christ? List ways in which we can see and know Christ.
Card 2	TRUSTING—BELIEVING John 14:5-14 What does this Scripture tell us about a relationship to Jesus Christ? List ways we can show our trust and belief.

Have pencils and Bibles available. Ask one person from each group to record and report the main points of its discussion.

Bring the group back together and share the findings. Try to discuss in practical ways the meaning of knowing, believing, and sharing with Christ.

CLOSING

Step 4: Closing (5 minutes)

The leader or another adult should share with the group members the meaning of his or her relationship with Jesus Christ. Briefly tell them about the beginning of it (how it came about), and emphasize how it has been necessary for that relationship to grow. Share some of your struggles and joys, a few of your doubts, but let them know that you are a human being and that you are working on making your relationship better. Communicate that none of us know all there is to know in this area. Close with prayer.

ADDITIONAL PROGRAM IDEAS

Another Closing

If you have extra time, include a prayer and meditation exercise at the end. This can be a very meaningful prayer time. It is best to use blindfolds; otherwise, have everyone close his or her eyes. Ask each to get comfortable on the floor, in a chair, or whatever. Then ask each to imagine himself or herself in a comfortable place, a place where each feels really good about himself or herself. Give them time. When all are "there" in their minds, have them imagine that

Jesus has stepped into the picture. "Jesus is there with you in the same place. In your mind go ahead and talk with Jesus. Listen to Jesus. Ask questions. Let your mind really get into a conversation with Jesus."

Allow two or three minutes for this, and when the time seems right, simply say, "You can begin to come back from your conversation. Open your eyes when you're ready." Wait for everyone to open his or her eyes.

Have some refreshments ready in another room, if possible, and share your experiences informally.

After Step 3

A. Try a faith history. Have everyone section off a sheet of paper so that each section is a period of life (preschool, grade school, junior high). Have each person list as many as possible of the influences, people, and events which have been important to his or her faith in each period.

B. Try a faith graph. Using the same periods of life mentioned above, have each person show the high points and low points in his or her relationship to Jesus in graph form.

C. Try a self-reflection exercise. Have each person mark on a continuum (from far away to very close) on a piece of paper the position which shows his or her relationship to Jesus today (see below).

_____

Far away   Very close

Then have him or her meditate for a brief time on ways in which he or she can move in the direction of greater closeness. Have each person work on this alone.

At the conclusion of the exercise, list on a large sheet of newsprint ways of moving in this direction of greater closeness to Christ. Encourage each person to commit himself or herself to one of the ways.

D. Have a time of sharing about people whom each person has known who have revealed Jesus Christ.

Franklin W. Nelson is the pastor of the First Baptist Church in Knoxville, Iowa. He has also been the associate pastor of the First Baptist Church, Davenport, Iowa, with special responsibilities for Christian education and youth ministries.

FAITH

having supper with Jesus

SIMULATING THE LAST SUPPER   Franklin W. Nelson

GOALS

To experience what it might have been like to be one of the followers of Jesus at his Last Supper, to learn more about the relationship Jesus had with people of his own day, and to learn that relationship with Jesus Christ means discipleship.

WHY?

Jesus takes on greater reality when one tries to experience him as those of the first century might have. Junior highs need to see more than just the divine Jesus far out in the clouds. They need to know the human Jesus on the cross. At a time when youth are so keenly aware of their own humanity, they are ripe and ready to relate to the humanity of Jesus. It is through his humanity that his divinity shows forth.

One of the most moving examples of the love of Jesus for his friends and one of the most revealing Scriptures about the person of Jesus is found in John 13–17. By reliving these last words of Christ to his disciples at the supper table, it is hoped that a junior high youth will learn what relationship to Christ involves.

This experience can work well with any number of youth and at any time of the year. However, the ideal size of the group would be ten to twenty-five, and the ideal time of the year would be right before Easter. The experience will have the greatest impact following a study of the life of Jesus and our relationship to him.

Much work and preparation go into a simulation experience like this, but the benefits can be very great as well. A simulation is really a grand role play. No great actors are required.

Mostly, the persons involved should be themselves, with the additional awareness of the characters they are trying to portray.

PREPARATION

Invitations

Send out invitations to the supper ahead of time. Be clever. Tell the youth the time, date (A.D. 30), and the place (the upper room at 506 Jerusalem Avenue). Ask them to come dressed casually.

The Room

Choose a room that will hold your group comfortably. Use tables that can be lowered, or place two folded tables, one on top of the other, with a tablecloth or sheet draped over them. Have the table large enough for at least thirteen people to be around it. Use pillows for seats. Have candles around the room for lighting. Have a basin and towel for washing hands or feet.

The Food

In order to be as authentic as possible, use such things as cheese, grapes, loaves of bread, olives, and grape juice. Spread the food on the table in baskets.

Music

Play music as the "disciples" arrive, such as *Jesus Christ Superstar, Godspell,* or some other contemporary record about the life and ministry of Jesus.

Name Tags

Prepare name tags for the followers of Jesus. On the reverse side of each tag should be information and/or Scriptures about the follower. Have Bibles available.

ANDREW—He was a good Jew who was a follower of John the Baptist and was looking eagerly for the Messiah to come to save the Jewish people. He was open and willing to learn. He had great enthusiasm. He was a fisherman by trade. John 1:35-42

PETER—He was a fisherman and a married man, the brother of Andrew. He was always named first among the disciples and was considered the leader of the disciples. He later became the leader of the church in Jerusalem after Jesus had ascended. Matthew 16:15-19; John 18:25-27

JOHN—He was a son of Zebedee and the younger brother of James. They were fishermen. He was one of the three apostles closest to Jesus. James and John were called the "sons of thunder." They were outspoken. Mark 10:35-41; Luke 9:51-56

PHILIP—He was a man from Bethsaida and perhaps a friend of the Greeks. He was one of the first disciples to be called by Jesus and then went to bring Nathanael to Jesus. John 1:43-49; 6:5-7; 12:20-23; 14:8-9

MATTHEW—He was a tax collector, wealthy, and probably despised by many people for his unfair dealings with people in the past. Matthew 9:9-13

JAMES—He was the older brother of John, one of the "sons of thunder." He was one of the top three leaders of the twelve disciples. He was a fisherman. Matthew 20:20-28

JAMES—He was the son of Alphaeus and one of the twelve disciples but is not mentioned except in the lists of the disciples. Matthew 10:3; Mark 3:18; Acts 1:13

JUDAS ISCARIOT—He was the betrayer of Jesus. He was the treasurer of the group. Why did he betray Jesus? Nobody knows. Matthew 26:14-16; John 12:3-6; 13:26-30

SIMON, THE PATRIOT—He was probably called the patriot because he identified himself with the fanatical opponents of Roman rule in Palestine. He was very patriotic about Judaism. Matthew 10:4

THOMAS—He was often called "Doubting Thomas"; but when evidence was produced, he was a strong believer, intensely loyal and brave. John 11:16; 14:5-6; 20:24-28

THADDAEUS—He was listed also as "Judas" (John 14:22-24). He was the son or brother of James (see Luke 6:16, RSV and KJV, respectively).

BARTHOLOMEW—He was known as one of the lesser apostles. He is mentioned by this name only in the listings of the Twelve. Many consider Bartholomew and Nathanael to be the same person. Matthew 10:3; Mark 3:18; Acts 1:13; John 1:45

Others:
  NICODEMUS—John 3:1-21; 7:47-52
  MARY OF BETHANY—Luke 10:38-42; John 11:1-44; 12:1-8
  MARTHA—Luke 10:38-42; John 11:1-44
  LAZARUS—John 11:1-44; 12:1-2, 9-11
  JOSEPH OF ARIMATHEA—Mark 15:42-47; John 19:38-42
  MARY, MOTHER OF JESUS—John 2:1-11; 20:11-18
  MARY MAGDALENE—Luke 8:1-3; Mark 15:40-41; John 20:11-18
  ZACCHAEUS—Luke 19:1-10
  THE BOY WITH THE FIVE LOAVES AND TWO FISH—John 6:1-14
  THE SAMARITAN WOMAN—John 4

Recruit someone to play the part of Jesus. The person who plays this role is a key in the success of the experience. He or she might be a pastor, an adult leader of the youth, or anyone in the congregation or community who could relate well to the youth in this assignment. (Or you yourself as leader may desire to play this part.)

PROCEDURE

Step 1

Meet the youth as they arrive at the doorway to the "upper room." Give each one a name tag. (Don't be too worried about females playing male parts, for this is only a role-play activity.) Instruct them to study the characters and Scripture passages for ten minutes or so. When each is ready to be that character, allow him or her to enter the room where the supper is being held. Have a sign at the door reading, "You are entering the first century." It might help, also, to have an instruction sign that says, "Be the disciple; feel, think, and act like the disciple."

Step 2

From this point on, the person playing Jesus, either you as leader or someone you have recruited, will lead the group. The following is directed to this person.

Be familiar with John 13–17. You may want to come dressed in costume with a robe and sandals. This may help your group to get into the spirit of the roles.

When each of your followers enters the room, wash his or her hands (or feet), using the basin of water and towel. Use a greeting such as "Shalom," and welcome each one by the name on his or her tag. Talk informally with one another. Have at least one other adult disciple in the room to help people mix easily. When all have arrived, gather around the table and begin the meal with the Lord's Prayer. Then begin eating.

At some point during the meal, in an informal way simply say, "This bread is like my body that is broken for you. Eat it and always remember me." Later during the meal, lift a glass of grape juice and say, "This is like the blood that I will shed for you. When you drink it, always remember me."

When the eating is about done, tell them that you have some important words to share with them, as you will be leaving them soon. You also have some instructions to give them.

For this next part you will need to be well prepared. Study John 13–17 and be able to paraphrase the portions of Scripture suggested below. If you choose not to use your own words, read from a modern translation. However, practice reading it so that it doesn't sound like it is being read.

During the pauses suggested below, there will be time for the "disciples" to respond to you or talk among themselves. There are some possible questions you might ask. The important thing is that you not be overly concerned if the youth choose not to speak. Silence in this experience will be very meaningful. Give them the chance to talk, but be careful not to insist.

Here is a possible sequence:
John 13:12b–17

"What are some ways you can serve me, and the Father who sent me, in the future?" Pause.
John 13:18-21b

Pause.
John 13:33-35

"In the past how have we shown love for one another?" Pause.

"Share among yourselves how you can show love for one another in the future." Pause.
John 14:6-7, 9-11

"Who do you think that I really am?" Pause.

"Do you remember some of the miracles you have seen?" Pause.
John 14:15-21

"Will you love me?" (Call on some of your disciples by name.) "How will you show me your love?" Pause.
John 14:27-29

"Have you found peace yet? Do you know what I'm talking about?" Pause.
John 15:5, 9-15

"Are you willing to lay down your lives for me? For a friend?" (Call on some of them by name.) Pause.
John 15:16-19

"How have you experienced the world's hate?"

Pause.
John 16:32-33

"My heart is heavy and burdened. Let's spend some time with our Father in prayer."
John 17:1b-5, 13-26

"It's time now to go to the garden to pray, but before we do, let me say one final word to you . . ." (have the group stand). Use Matthew 28:18b-20.

Greet as many of the disciples as you possibly can and then leave the room together.

OTHER ENDINGS

You might want to sing a simple hymn that the whole group would know, such as "God Is So Good," "Alleluia," or "Amazing Grace." After the hymn the group would leave.

You may want to invite the group to share expressions of love, such as handshakes, hugs, or last words of farewell.

You may find it necessary to end the experience by gathering the group members in another room for a brief time of sharing and reacting to the experience. Ask them:

What was the most meaningful part for you?

What was the most important thing you learned?

What do you suppose were some of the feelings the friends of Jesus had when they saw him on the cross?

What are some ways we can be disciples of Jesus in today's world?

How have we in the past shown our love for one another?

How can we do a better job in the future?

ADDITIONAL PROGRAM IDEAS

Try an intergenerational supper. Invite some other adults to share in the meal. This would work especially well with smaller youth groups.

Have one or two of the youth share their experience in the church newsletter or during the next Communion worship service.

Invite another youth group from a church of a different denomination to share in the experience. Then follow up the experience by doing a comparative study of Communion in both church traditions.

Do a study of Communion in your own church tradition. You may want to ask a pastor, deacon, or elder to share in the study with you.

Franklin W. Nelson is pastor of the First Baptist Church of Knoxville, Iowa. He has also been the associate pastor at the First Baptist Church in Davenport, Iowa, with special responsibilities in Christian education and youth ministries.

FAITH

would anyone care if I were dead?

FACING DEATH   Everett A. Denniston

If I can help somebody as I pass along,
if I can cheer somebody with a word or song,
If I can show somebody he is traveling wrong,
then my living will not be in vain.
If I can do my duty as a Christian ought,
if I can bring salvation to a world once wrought,
if I can spread the message as the Master taught,
Then my living will not be in vain.

Only very recently—in the last few years—has the phenomenon of death begun to be talked about openly. As a youth-worshiping culture we tend to deny and even repress thoughts of death and dying, a taboo never broached. Now at last the silence about death is being broken, and a new openness toward the subject of death is being felt, particularly in the educational fields. As Christian educators we have a responsibility to speak of the meaning of Christian hope: to proclaim the power that is available in Christ to face and deal with the vital issues of life, especially that of death; to help create an atmosphere of acceptance and understanding in which the meaning, purpose, and value of life can be questioned and affirmed; and to speak of the great promise of resurrection and life after death that is the foundation of New Testament teaching about death.

It is important to understand that to guide youth in facing death, one must be in touch with the fact of his or her own eventual death. To help them affirm the value of life and our hope in Christ is only possible if we have realistically faced our own death and thus can help create that atmosphere of trust in which youth can talk about death openly and honestly. You are the key here; as they see you living out your faith authentically, honestly dealing with your own fears and doubts, you become a model for their own faith ventures. Pray about your leadership—that God's Spirit will bring important new dimensions to the lives of your junior highs as they face their own deaths and that they will know a peace, a comfort, and a strength in trusting their lives to God.

GOALS

1. To give an opportunity for junior high youth to think and talk about death—and principally their own deaths—within a supportive faith community.

2. To explore the biblical resources that speak of the Christian hope in resurrection and life after death.

3. To explore, affirm, and celebrate that which gives meaning to one's own life as a gift from God.

CREATING PERSONALIZED NAME TAGS

> ### WHY?
>
> This exercise builds community through personal acquaintance and sharing. It also helps youth to think in terms of self-identity: who they and others are beyond just their names.

Preparation

Materials needed: construction paper (different colors)
scissors
felt-tipped pens
yarn cut into three-foot lengths

Procedure

Have each person in the group—including leaders—make his or her own name tag by cutting it out of construction paper. The shape should identify something important about that person; for example, a person really into skateboarding might cut a name tag in the shape of a skateboard and use a felt-tipped pen to finish the likeness. Interests and moods of junior highs change often enough that this exercise can be used frequently, giving both youth and adult leaders insight into one another. It also brings new people on board faster. Give youth a few minutes to share their name tags with one another around the group. This also gets them talking about themselves which will be important in the exercise to follow.

EXPLORING FEELINGS ABOUT DEATH

WHY?

It's easy, particularly when we are young, to avoid our feelings about death. But death does touch many young lives—perhaps through a classmate, an elderly relative, or even a parent. The first step toward developing a Christian view of death is to recognize our current feelings and questions, whether positive or negative.

Preparation

Materials needed: paper
pencils
crayons
construction paper
glue
old magazines
scissors

Procedure

Ask the youth to do one of the following:
A. write a poem
B. draw a picture
C. make a collage
D. write a letter to God

Tell them that this should express their concepts, feelings, questions, and doubts about death. Tell them also that there will be an opportunity to share the finished product with the group but that no one will be forced to share if he or she doesn't want to do so. Ask them to work quietly and individually; then have them share what they have prepared with the entire group or in groups of three or four.

EXPLORING THE BIBLICAL RESOURCES

The Scriptures continually speak of death not as the end of life, but as its beginning. And so the Christian has nothing to fear from death; our victory is in Christ Jesus, our Lord. Any good topical concordance, such as *Nave's Topical Concordance* or *Harper's Topical Bible,* will reveal an abundance of passages on resurrection.

1. If you have access to several topical concordances, divide your group into smaller ones and have them search out with the help of the concordances Scriptures that speak of the Christian's hope in resurrection. Give each small group time to find several; then have a time for the groups to report back to the whole group those that they found and the significance of them for their lives. (You might ask them to respond to the question: "How should we then live, according to these passages?")

2. If you have no such access to these concordances, pick several well-known biblical passages which speak of resurrection (at least one for each small group), such as John 3:16; Romans 8:35-39; 1 Corinthians 6:14; 15:1-58; and Ephesians 2:4-6. Divide your group into smaller groups, give each one a passage, and ask the group to discuss it in light of these two questions: (*a*) What is the passage basically saying? (*b*) What does it mean to me; how does the hope it gives affect my life now? When each group is finished, or after a predetermined length of time (about ten minutes), have each group in turn report its findings to the total group. Long Scripture passages, such as 1 Corinthians 15, should be broken down into several smaller ones.

WRITING ONE'S OWN EULOGY

WHY?

This experience gives each youth an opportunity to express what he or she wants his or her life to stand for and confronts each with the necessity to find meaning in his or her own life and to look at where that meaning is to be found.

Procedure

(1) Distribute paper and pencils to each member of the group. (2) Ask each to write his or her own eulogy. (Explain what a eulogy is.) For what do they want to be remembered? What do they want to have said at their

funerals? You might read as an example the quotation at the very beginning of this activity. (3) If you feel they would be comfortable in doing so, have each person share his or her eulogy with another member of the group.

CELEBRATION

It is hoped that this has been a positive time together, focused on the hope that is ours in Christ Jesus to overcome death. Now CELEBRATE this time together for a few minutes any way that is celebration for your group. Here are a few suggestions: (1) read aloud a meaningful Scripture passage and together verbally respond with "PRAISE GOD"; (2) sing together a song of celebration; (3) have several youth say what this time together has meant to them personally, what joy they have found in it; (4) have youth read together the quotation and respond together verbally, as above. Whatever way you choose to celebrate, be sure to close together in prayer, thanking God for the gift of life to each of you each day and for Christ's victory over death that brings us the promise of eternal life with God.

ADDITIONAL PROGRAM IDEAS

Guided Fantasy

Editor's note: Fantasy exercises are very effective in helping others get in touch with their deep feelings about death, but this should be used only if the leader has had experience with this particular tool and if someone with counseling skills can be present. Also, the group should be fairly mature and stable.

WHY?

This exercise allows youth in a nonthreatening way to review past experiences and visualize their own deaths and funerals. It can get them in touch with feelings about death and what has and will be significant in their lives.

Procedure for the Fantasy

1. This must be done in a serious mood. Ask youth to get comfortable, relax, close their eyes, and let their minds wander. No talking.

2. After a few moments to let them get into the proper mood, ask them to think back to their early childhood. What experiences do they remember? (Think, not talk.) What do they remember about their family members, the house(s) and neighborhood(s) they lived in? Who were their friends? What do they remember about school? Teachers? Classmates? Any girl friends or boy friends? Are the feelings positive or negative as they think about these things?

3. After a sufficient amount of time to process these thoughts, ask the youth to think into the future, as they graduate from high school. What do they see themselves doing? Perhaps they are going on to college (What is it like? Where do they go to college?) or getting a job (Doing what?). What about marriage? If they are going to get married, what do their partners look like? Any children? What else do they see themselves doing as they grow older?

4. Now ask the youth to experience themselves as they grow much older and to imagine the time of their deaths. How old are they? How does it happen? Are they ready to die? Is it a peaceful experience or a frightening one?

5. Now they are going to their own funerals; as they walk into the funeral home, whom do they see? Who is there? Their parents? Friends (which ones)? Are they crying or at peace? Everyone is filing by the casket now, and as the youth look in to see themselves, what do they look like? How old are they? What are their feelings?

6. Now the minister gets up to speak; what does he or she say? What have the lives of the youth been about? Does the minister mention particular people they have known? The work of the youth? Their church? What have they stood for in their lives? How do the youth feel about what the minister had to say? How do the people react?

7. Now they go with the funeral procession to the graveside. The words of committal are spoken, and they are lowered into the ground. The group begins to break up. How do they feel about their funerals? Was what they want said spoken? Were the right people there? Are they at peace?

8. Now have them slowly begin to come back to the present. They feel themselves traveling back through time, from the future to the present. They feel life within their bodies again. When they are ready, they may open their eyes and see what is around them.

Debrief the Fantasy

Have youth reflect on and discuss the experience. Help them to focus on their feelings, to go beyond what they actually saw in the fantasy. Was it pleasant or scary? What did they appreciate most about what happened? What would they like to change? Did they feel good about their lives? Were they meaningful and fulfilled? (What made or did not make them so?) What was left undone? What would they change? Did their deaths feel real to them? Do they have any thoughts about what follows death? Ask them the question: "WOULD ANYONE CARE IF YOU WERE DEAD? WHO? WHY?"

Other Program Ideas

1. Ask youth to think about and respond to the question: "How would you spend your life if you knew you had only six months to live?"

2. Have youth write a prayer to God, expressing their feelings about death and God's promise of eternal life.

3. Have youth imagine they have been spared from death by some great miracle (perhaps they lived through a tragic accident or a heart attack). Then have them think about for what purpose they were spared. What are the reasons for their lives? How are they to go about finding God's direction for their lives from that point on?

SUGGESTIONS FOR FOLLOW-UP PROGRAMS

1. Visit a cemetery; this can be quite enlightening. Notice particularly the expressions of hope written on grave markers, especially in older cemeteries.

2. Take your youth through a funeral home; this can be arranged with a local mortician.

3. Together attend a funeral; check with your pastor.

4. Ask your pastor to talk to your youth group about funerals and his or her counseling with bereaved families.

5. Get in touch with a doctor, chaplain, or psychologist who works with dying patients. Ask him or her to speak to your group about his or her experiences, emphasizing the hope he or she has seen in the faces of dying patients.

RESOURCES

There are dozens of good books on the subject of death and dying. Some that I have been in touch with are the following:

Doss, Richard W., *The Last Enemy: A Theology of Death.* New York: Harper & Row, Publishers, 1974.

Jackson, Edgar N., *Telling a Child About Death.* New York: Hawthorn Books, Inc., 1965.

Kübler-Ross, Elisabeth, ed., *Death—The Final Stage of Growth.* Englewood Cliffs, N.J.: Prentice-Hall, Inc., 1975.

Kübler-Ross, Elisabeth, *On Death and Dying.* New York: Macmillan, Inc., 1969.

LeShan, Eda, *Learning to Say Good-by: When a Parent Dies.* New York: Macmillan, Inc., n.d.

Lund, Doris, *Eric.* New York: Dell Publishing Co., Inc., 1975.

Moody, Raymond A., Jr., *Life After Life.* New York: Bantam Books, Inc., 1976.

——————, *Reflections on Life After Life.* New York: Two Continents Publishing Group, Inc., 1977.

Rev. Everett A. Denniston is associate pastor at Eastwood Baptist Church in Medford, Oregon, with special responsibilities in educational ministries.

FEELINGS
FEELINGS
FEELINGS

FEELINGS

FEELINGS

I love me

EXPERIENCING SELF-WORTH   **Margaret S. English**

GOAL

To enable each person in the group to feel his or her innate worth.

WHY?

The ability to tread lightly between conformity and individuality is an important skill for successful living. For junior highs there are special struggles between pressures from parents and teachers and from their own age group. One asset during this struggle is a genuine feeling of self-worth. The church can play a major role in developing this love of self. So much of the time religious instruction emphasizes loving others, forgetting that Jesus coupled this instruction with "you shall love your neighbor as yourself" (Matthew 22:39). This program concentrates on this basic requirement.

One reason people do love themselves (and treat themselves with respect) is that they feel unique and believe their lives have meaning and purpose. Junior highs are beginning to explore such purposes and realize their unique gifts. Churches can provide opportunities to evaluate these purposes and gifts in a Christian context.

This program uses some psychological theories related to Transactional Analysis to help junior highs analyze their own personalities. Realizing why we act or feel the way we do is an important step in self-awareness. No one is ever too young to begin the process.

PREPARATION

The leader should try out the "I'm OK—You're OK" theory in his or her mind before attempting to explain it to the group. It is a simple and quick way of seeing how inner attitudes can affect the way we feel about ourselves and our relationships with others. Some books are listed below which will aid in understanding the theory. It is hoped, however, that the explanation given here will be sufficient for your use. It might be helpful to list and describe the four basic relationships listed in Step 2 on a large sheet of newsprint or chalkboard so that everyone can see them as the discussion goes on.

Before the meeting, instruct someone to make notes on the reactions from the audience during Step 1.

Get a recording of "Make Your Own Kind of Music." This is a song which was popular within the past few years.

PROCEDURE

Step 1 (15 minutes)

The leader should begin the meeting by saying something like, "I'm very happy you're here tonight. I have a program planned which should be very interesting. I spent a lot of time preparing it, and I think I have learned things that will interest you." Proceed with statements about what unique talents and experiences make you (the leader) a worthwhile and useful person. Do not compare yourself with others. Do not make statements like "I'm the best . . . ," "Compared to . . . ," or "My friends say. . . ." Keep it nonjudgmental and free of outside comparison. In other words, "lay it on thick." It is *most* important that whatever the leader says is sincere and thought out. The impact will be lost if the leader is uncomfortable or unrealistic. One has to have a sincere self-respect if this is to succeed.

Reactions to this speech may be close to nausea. There may be disbelief or joking. Have a person act as recorder and unobtrusively make notes of various comments. When the leader is finished, allow the group members to talk about their reactions. Let the recorder be a starting point and resource. You may use the following questions:

1. What was your initial reaction? Did it change as you listened to more of the leader's speech?
2. Did you feel the leader was being honest?
3. Did it make you feel bad about yourself to hear such self-praise from another? Did it hurt anyone else's feelings? Was there an "I'm-better-than-you" attitude?
4. Why do we react so strongly to "bragging"?
5. What does it mean to be humble? From what does that protect us?
6. What does it mean to be loving?
7. What did Jesus say about loving oneself? (See Mark 12:31.)
8. Have you ever been mad at yourself and taken it out on someone else? (Like flunking an exam and later telling your sister she's a dummy.) Think of examples.

Step 2 (10 minutes)

Discuss briefly the idea that what we feel about ourselves does affect the way we treat others. The way others treat us also affects how we feel about ourselves. Some psychologists say that we have developed basic attitudes toward ourselves and others, and they use these terms which are easy to understand:

"I'm OK—You're OK"—When people take this position, everyone is happy and treated well.

"I'm not OK—You're OK"—This position often results in envy, jealousy, and insecurity. It can also cause people to look for situations which confirm this feeling of inferiority.

"I'm OK—You're not OK"—This results in inhuman behavior, snobbishness, misused authority, even crimes in which someone is victimized (because he or she is "not OK").

"I'm not OK—You're not OK"—This occurs rarely, and it leaves no avenue for hope. Mental illness and suicide are possible because all of life is useless from this position.

Step 3 (15 minutes)

Hand out pencils and paper. Ask individuals to spend one minute writing down all the reasons they think they're OK. Inevitably there is someone who can't think of anything to write. This is a good opportunity to encourage the rest of the group to help him or her think of good traits.

Divide into groups of three. Instruct two people to listen without comment while one talks. Let them decide who goes first. Allow each person to spend one minute talking about his or her good qualities or unique traits. The listeners can provide encouragement with nods or smiles but may not speak until the time is up. This is an exercise not only in liking oneself but also in listening without criticism. After all have finished, allow the group members a minute to discuss their reactions. Collect the lists made earlier, and save them for the next meeting.

Step 4 (5 minutes)

End with the theme song for the program, "Make Your Own Kind of Music"; either play a recording of it or, if he or she sings well, let someone sing it. Then read Leviticus 19:17-18.

ADDITIONAL PROGRAM IDEAS

After Step 2 divide into groups of no more than five, and assign each group a Bible story to analyze according to the "I'm OK—You're OK" patterns just discussed. Some suggestions are: Joseph and his brothers (Genesis 37), Jacob and Esau (Genesis 25:27-34), the good Samaritan (Luke 10:29-37), breaking of the sabbath (Mark 2:23-28), and the prodigal son (Luke 15:11-32). Have each small group share its conclusions with the total group.

RESOURCES

Harris, Thomas A., *I'm OK—You're OK: A Practical Guide to Transactional Analysis.* New York: Harper & Row, Publishers, Inc., 1967.

James, Muriel, and Jongeward, Dorothy, *Born to Win: Transactional Analysis with Gestalt Experiments.* Reading, Mass.: Addison-Wesley Publishing Co., Inc., 1971.

James, Muriel, *Born to Love: Transactional Analysis in the Church.* Reading, Mass.: Addison-Wesley Publishing Co., Inc., 1973.

Margaret S. English has been a junior high fellowship sponsor in the First Baptist Church of Billings, Montana, and she has been co-director of the state camp for junior-high-aged American Baptists.

FEELINGS

different strokes for different folks

GIVING AND RECEIVING SUPPORT THROUGH STROKES   Margaret S. English

Editor's note: This program uses material presented in the previous program. If you are not going to use both programs in this sequence, you'll want to devise a way to present the basic concepts from "I Love Me."

GOALS

To grow in the ability to give and receive support and admiration and to become aware of our strengths as others see them.

WHY?

We all need to be respected. Yet we can all identify with the comedian who says, "I don't get no respect." Ironically, often the things persons need the most are most difficult to give. All of us need to know how others perceive our strengths, and we need to help them perceive theirs. This session will concentrate on expressing our appreciation and love of others. These techniques have been used before, but they never grow old, and the results are amazing. They can turn a hostile, uncooperative group into fast friends. In fact, the group might benefit from incorporating some of these exercises into every meeting. They send everyone home feeling good about himself or herself and others.

PREPARATION

Bring along a stuffed animal—preferably one that has had long, loving use. The lists of "I'm OKs" from the previous session will be used. Also, a recording of one of the songs listed at the end of this session will be needed.

PROCEDURE

Step 1 (10 minutes)

Have the group form a circle. (If the group is large, you may need two circles.) Place the stuffed animal in the center of the circle. Introduce it and tell the group this is its new pet. Ask each person to go to the pet and make it feel loved and welcome. Encourage the group members to express physically and verbally their appreciation of the new pet. (E.g., "Gee, that's a cute button nose," or "You sure are cuddly.") They can stroke it, hug it, dance it around. Don't worry if they laugh and joke or feel uncomfortable. That's part of getting over the discomfort of saying "mushy" things in front of others.

After all have had an opportunity to express their feeling to the pet, allow for discussion of the term "strokes." Some questions you could use are:

1. What are some other names for compliments, or strokes? ("Warm fuzzies" comes to mind.)
2. How do you usually give strokes? Is it difficult for you?
3. How do you react to strokes?

Step 2: Role Play (5 minutes)

Briefly review the attitudes discussed in the last session. Divide six people into three pairs. Have three pairs of young people act out (one pair at a time) the following role-play situations while the rest of the group observes. Instruct one person from the pair to give a positive stroke. The second will respond according to one of the following positions:

—I'm OK—You're not OK (I don't need your stroke).

—I'm not OK—You're OK (I don't deserve that).

—I'm OK—You're OK (Thanks, I needed that).

Allow a few minutes to discuss times when people have reacted these ways.

Step 3 (10 minutes)

Divide into groups of three. You might want to return to the small groups formed in the previous session, if possible. Have one person remain silent while the other two give him or her strokes. Allow one to two minutes per person depending on how mature the groups are. Allow them time to discuss their reactions.

Step 4 (10 minutes)

Pass out the lists from the previous session. Remaining in groups of three, compare those lists with what people said during the "strokes" session (Step 2). Let them share as much of their original lists as they wish. Consider the following questions:

1. Are the lists similar to the strokes?
2. If not, why not? Are you afraid of being yourself and showing your strong points? Do you fear rejection because your strong points aren't good enough? Does the group know you well enough?
3. Do you sometimes have the "I'm OK—You're not OK" or the "I'm not OK—You're OK" attitude? Can you do anything to change that? Can the two people in your group help? Have they helped?

Step 5 (10 minutes)

Read 1 Corinthians 13:1-13 responsively. The leader reads the "if" portions, and the group responds with the "but have not love" portions. Then the leader reads the "love is" portions, with the group responding with the "it is not" portions. Alternate on verses seven through twelve, and read the final verse in unison. Although some might have difficulty following along, it is important that they use their Bibles rather than a typewritten sheet since the former conveys the Bible's versatility.

Close the meeting by singing together "Charity" which is based on this chapter. If your group is not familiar with that song, close with a popular tune which expresses appreciation for others (e.g., "You've Made Me So Very Happy" or "You've Got a Friend").

ADDITIONAL PROGRAM IDEA

Between Steps 1 and 2 replace the stuffed animal with a person from the group. Ask the members of the group to express, one at a time, physically—using no words—how they feel about the person in the center. This expression may be a hug, a handshake, a gentle (make this clear to everyone) sock in the arm, a dance—whatever. Talk over how it felt. Did everyone think about how he or she really felt about the person in the center, or did he or she just do what the person before had done? Was it hard to keep silent? Did the person feel an "I'm OK—You're OK" attitude?

Margaret S. English has been a junior high fellowship sponsor in the First Baptist Church of Billings, Montana. She has also been co-director of the state camp for junior-high-aged American Baptists.

FEELINGS

beauty or the beast?

EXAMINING BEAUTY STANDARDS   **Margaret S. English**

GOAL

To examine beauty as depicted in the media and explore other standards of beauty.

WHY?

Advertisers put a heavy burden on us to conform to their standards of physical beauty. By examining their motives, perhaps we will not succumb so easily to the ploy. However, we need to clarify which values we hold higher than the media's. The following program will deal with these issues. Can we appreciate one another's unique beauty and differing tastes regardless of the media? This program hopes to help youth answer, "Yes."

PREPARATION

Materials needed: current magazines (preferably geared to teenagers) to cut up
paste
two large pieces of newsprint or poster board
words or a recording of the song "Everything Is Beautiful"

PROCEDURE

Step 1 (10 minutes)

Divide into two groups. One group is assigned to make an "ugly" poster. This should be a collage of all the disasters which advertising and the media in general imply make us ugly (pimples, greasy hair, fat, etc.). The other group will make a "beautiful" poster. Include all the products which make teeth whiter, hair shinier, skin tanner, etc. Also, include stereotypically "beautiful" or "ugly" men and women. Display the posters and let them be discussed.

Step 2 (10 minutes)

Have a thumbs-up, thumbs-down vote on the following characteristics (thumbs up means you approve; thumbs down means you disapprove):
—long hair on girls/short hair on girls
—long hair on boys/short hair on boys
—eyeglasses
—eye makeup on girls
—big muscles on boys
—blue jeans in church
Let the group get in the act and select its own characteristics.

Step 3 (10 minutes)

Have each person in the group think of or write down the name of a person he or she knows personally whom he or she admires and respects—not necessarily for his or her looks. Is he or she beautiful by the standards just expressed in the poster and by the vote? Ask the following questions:
—If the person is beautiful, what difference does it make personally in his or her relationships? Is physical beauty ever a handicap?
—Does he or she ever have the "uglies"? How does that affect him or her personally in his or her relationships?
—How about you? Do your friends treat you differently when you have pimples or forget to brush your teeth?
—Do you like to be around only good-looking people? What is important in relationships with others?
—How would you feel if someone came to you and said something like, "You ought to do something about those pimples"?

Step 4 (15 minutes)

Teach the group a new game called "You're beautiful." This is similar to the old "Pack my bag for China" game except the person who begins turns to the person on his or her left and says, "You're beautiful because . . . (your hair is a pretty color; I like the way you dress; you have a smile that lights up the room; etc.)." The person just complimented repeats, "I'm beautiful because. . . ," then turns to his or her left and tells his or her neighbor why he or she, in turn, is beautiful. The catch is that each person down the line must remember and repeat why everyone else before him or her is beautiful.

Close by singing or listening to "Everything Is Beautiful."

ADDITIONAL PROGRAM IDEA

(This can be used in place of Step 3 or between Steps 3 and 4.) If the group has two articulate members, you might want to try a debate. The leader should meet with them ahead of time to help them plan strategy. The issue can be "Resolved: Christians should not wear makeup or take unnatural interest in their personal appearance"; or "Resolved: Christians should do everything possible to look attractive in the eyes of others." Give each side one to two minutes to present its arguments. Allow the same amount of time for each to give a rebuttal. Encourage the sides to use Bible verses to strengthen their arguments. Some suggestions could include 1 Samuel 16:7; Colossians 2:8; Romans 8:5-8; Luke 12:27; Matthew 6:28; Romans 14:13-14; 1 Corinthians 6:19-20. Let the group members vote on the winner of the debate and then on which side they personally support.

Margaret S. English served three years as a junior high fellowship sponsor in the First Baptist Church of Billings, Montana. She also co-directed a state-wide camp for junior-high-aged American Baptists.

FEELINGS

left out

FEELING LEFT OUT AND LONELY   **Lillian (Biviano) Barron**

GOAL

Through this program junior highs will learn about the importance of positive, loving actions toward themselves and others who are lonely and left out.

WHY?

All of us hate to feel "left out" of the crowd. This is especially true of junior-high-aged youth who are struggling to understand themselves in relation to others. There is a tendency in all of us to be hard on those who do not seem "to belong" in our group because of personality, color, social background, or different mannerisms. This program is designed to help both the "left out" and those who "leave out" others increase their understanding of the problems involved.

PREPARATION

Prepare a poster board or bulletin board with clippings from a newspaper or magazine which illustrate situations in which some people seem to be outsiders and situations in which some people seem to be insiders. These might be a child left out (or included) at play, refugees waiting for admittance to another country, an incident of racial discrimination, a classroom, sports picture, etc. Use these pictures on your wall to create interest in the topic. They may also be used as a basis for a discussion.

PROCEDURE

Game

Ask everyone but one person to stand in a circle holding hands. The "outsider" is to try to get into the circle. The circle members do everything they can to prevent the outsider from getting into the circle (move closer together, keep legs together, cross arms, etc.). Repeat this three or four times with different "outsiders." Take about ten minutes for this.

Discussion

When the game is finished, sit down on the floor in a circle and discuss some of the feelings group members had. Take about ten minutes to do this.
1. How did the "outsider" feel after trying so hard to get into the circle and failing to do so?
2. How did the circle members feel about not letting the "outsider" into the circle? Was anyone tempted to allow an opening? Did anyone allow an opening?
3. Did any "outsider" get into the circle in spite of the blocking? If so, how did he or she feel?
4. Relate this experience to our everyday lives.

Role Playing

Divide the group into four small groups. Ask each group to plan one of the role plays:
1. A group of junior high youth are excitedly talking about (and planning) a party. On the sideline is a dejected person who is obviously being left out.
2. A boy or a girl asks several peers of the opposite sex to go with him or her to a school event and is refused by each one asked.
3. Jeff is not a new boy in the youth group, but he doesn't feel that he belongs. The others don't seem to want to make him feel welcome.
4. Angela, a new girl in the neighborhood, speaks with a foreign accent. She is having trouble understanding her schoolwork. She stops at Sarah's house to ask to borrow a textbook which

she forgot to bring home. Sarah has some friends visiting but gives Angela the book. No one greets Angela or invites her to join them.

Discussion

Talk about *each* situation and try to feel what the "left out" person was feeling.
1. How does it feel to be left out of a group while it is planning?
2. What does it feel like to receive so many "no's" from the opposite sex?
3. How could members of the youth group really make Jeff feel welcome? What more is needed than simply being polite?
4. What do you think Angela really wanted from Sarah? What more did Angela need from Sarah and her friends? Why was giving the book not enough to do?

Closure

Read Luke 10:25-37, the parable of the good Samaritan. Jesus, a Jew, was telling this parable to other Jews in answer to the question "Who is my neighbor?" Although he does not say it, it has usually been assumed that the victim was a Jew, also. The priest and Levite, the most respected types of Jews, would not spend their time and energy to help a fellow Jew. It was a Samaritan, one of a group hated by the Jews and considered inferior, who had compassion on him. That a Samaritan would help a Jew (who under other circumstances might not even acknowledge his existence) was a sign of great caring.

Discuss: How did the Samaritan help?
1. He was willing to become personally involved.
2. He cared about the man as a person.
3. He was basically concerned and alert to the needs of the man.
4. He symbolizes Christ and Christ's love reaching out to others.

How can we help persons to know that they are really on the "inside"?

Prayer

Accept or Except, Lord?*

Lord, I like to think that I accept everyone for what they are. But if I really get honest, I'd have to say that I accept everyone with exceptions.

What I mean to say is that it's easy to love and accept everyone in general. But it's a little harder for me to accept an individual who's standing next to me whom I can't seem to really like because of some peculiarity or habit.

But it's not a laughing matter, is it, Lord? I need help in accepting the unacceptable (by my standards, anyway). I need help in seeing all people the way You see all people.

Lord, give me Your eyes when I look at people. Give me Your love when I must deal with all types of people. Give me Your patience to understand and accept the people around me, like parents and friends and teachers, neighbors, salesmen, bus drivers, and little brothers.

I know You accept me as I am, Lord. Thanks.

Now let me see people Cross-eyed—as I look at them through Your death and resurrection for me. Then, and only then, can I really accept the people You have put into my daily life!

ADDITIONAL PROGRAM IDEAS

1. Set up two tasks to be completed in the meeting session—one achievable, one not achievable. (You might use two questionnaires about factual information. One group is allowed to use resources which are provided. The other group must rely on its own memory and learning.) Give a time limit to complete the task. Discuss this experience together. The group that fails will want to let off a lot of steam with the group that succeeds. Let the members express how they feel, what they want to do about their failure, how they feel toward the group that had the resources. How can this experience help them understand others in relation to daily situations of success and failure? (Note: This approach could take the place of the role playing.)

2. Additional Bible study, Matthew 25:31-46: With this passage consider our Christian concern for others. The passage tells us that Jesus helps us see the needs of the lonely and tells us what to do about them.

*Richard Bimler, *Pray, Praise and Hooray* (St. Louis, Mo.: Concordia Publishing House, 1972), p. 16.

Lillian (Biviano) Barron is a free-lance curriculum writer and local church Christian educator in Carnegie, Pennsylvania. She has been a director of Christian education and a director of youth ministries. Ms. Barron has also assisted with youth conferences and Christian education workshops.

FEELINGS

2bs + 2cs = failure

DEALING INTERGENERATIONALLY WITH FAILURE IN SCHOOL   Lillian (Biviano) Barron

GOAL

Through this program junior high youth and their parents will have an opportunity to share their thoughts about report cards, achievements, and expectations of each other. This is an inter-generational program dealing with failure in school and parental pressure to achieve.

WHY?

Parents' concern for the school progress of their junior highers may lead to problems between the youth and parents. Each youth is trying to decide who he or she is, how to adjust to the school situation, and just what he or she wants to achieve in life. Parents are concerned that their children achieve good grades not only in preparation for high school and life in general but also sometimes as a reflection upon themselves and their abilities. Sometimes parents put a great deal of pressure on their children to do well, and the youth are not able or perhaps are not willing to accept another definition of what they should accomplish or be. The bitterness, hurt, and anger from these conflicts can be very destructive to family relationships.

PREPARATION

Two weeks in advance, invite parents (make invitations, organize a telephone committee, or have certain youths call an assigned group of parents). Assign someone to prepare light refreshments. Make simulations of report cards on newsprint and hang them on the walls in the meeting room. Have newsprint or chalkboard available.

PROCEDURE

Have a junior high host and hostess greet the parents. Open the meeting with a few words of welcome to everyone, and brief the group on the plans for the evening.

Get Acquainted

Grading the parents! Have the letters *A, B, C, D, F* on sheets of paper on the floor. As each of the situations from the list below is read, each youth is to go to the sheet of paper which best indicates the grade he or she would give to his or her parents.

1. My parents treat me as though I'm a junior higher.
2. My parents understand me.
3. My parents are with it (think in today's terms).
4. My parents try to keep good family relationships.
5. My mother/father is a good cook.
6. My mother/father leaves work problems at work.
7. My parents are fair in their expectations of me.
8. My parents keep their room neat.

Grading the youth! Parents will now grade their junior highers on the following items:

1. My junior higher is as responsible and helpful as he or she should be.
2. My child keeps his or her room neat.
3. My child is considerate of other members of the family.
4. My youth is fair in his or her expectations of me.
5. My junior higher does his or her homework.
6. My child is a good cook.
7. My youth keeps me in line when I need it.
8. My junior higher is a good money saver.

(You may make up a list of your own. Try not to

select anything which would be too judgmental or embarrassing. Remember, this is all in fun!)

Role Playing

Separate the parents and youth. Ask the parents to plan and role-play how they would react if their child brought home a report card with grades not up to their expectations. There may be varying reactions, ranging from anger to encouragement, which would lead to more than one role play.

Ask the youth to plan and role-play what would happen if they brought home report cards with grades lower than what their parents expect them to receive. What would they say to their friends? What would they plan to tell their parents? What reactions would they expect from their parents?

Respond to Role Playing

After both groups are finished, discuss what happened in each situation, what some feelings were, what differences were noted by parents and youth, and how true to life the role playing really was. If parents and youth can be honest, there is a possibility for fruitful discussion at this time. You may choose to conduct the discussion in one large group or in small groups of eight or ten youths and parents combined. If you plan to use small groups, consider ahead of time whether or not it would be helpful to have parents and their children in the same small group. This depends on the maturity of both youth and parents.

Intergenerational Role Playing

Divide into two groups for the following role plays. Include both youth and adults in each group.
1. September—Parents are talking with their child about their expectations of the youth, putting on pressure to do really well in school.
2. November (first report period ends)—Youth takes home a report card. Have family consultation discussing the report card and school activities.

Discussion

First, divide into small groups to discuss the following questions; then gather in the large group to share the results. Write your conclusions on newsprint.

1. What are some ways parents might act in family situations such as this one to bring about better understanding between parents and teenagers?
2. What are some ways in which teenagers might act to bring about better understanding between themselves and their parents?
3. Why is it important for us as Christian young people and as Christian parents to have good relationships in our families?

Closure

Read Colossians 3:12-14 in unison. Think about what Paul says is important for Christians who live and worship together. What is important in family decisions about poor grades or failure? Read 2 Timothy 2:15 (RSV) together and reflect silently on it. Ask, "Do I present myself to God as a workman who has no need to be ashamed?" Let each answer the question silently.

Have someone read the following prayer:

Are We Making the Grade with You?*

What are school grades, Lord? How important are they in Your life?

In my life they are very important. I need good grades to continue my education, to be eligible for school organizations and the football team. My parents demand that I bring home nothing worse than a *B*. I am ranked according to my grade-point average.

Sometimes I think grades are really overdone. I have even been tempted to cheat, just so I can keep up with my grades. Too many people put too much emphasis on them. Right now I may not be getting a very good education, but I sure am getting good grades!

Do You grade me too, Lord, each day? Did I fail yesterday because I was in a horrible mood? Or what about last Wednesday when I lost my temper at my dad?

Do You have a grading system something like this:

I get an *A* for helping a grandma across the street.
I get a *B* if I take the garbage out.
I get a *C* if I forget to clean my room sometimes.
I get a *D* if I come in late from a date.
I get an *F* if I don't do anything worthwhile some day.

I can't believe that You would fail anyone, Lord. That's what my faith tells me. I mean, how does a person fail life?

Lord, help me to do two things: Help me to keep grades in the right perspective. Help others too. And also help me to see that Your love for me is always *A*+. That You always

*Richard Bimler, *Pray, Praise and Hooray* (St. Louis, Mo.: Concordia Publishing House, 1972), pp. 96-97.

look at me as Your "favorite pupil." That You look at everyone that way.

There are people around me that look like they have failed life. Let me "bring up their grade" by showing them concern and forgiveness.

Lord, with You I've made the grade. Because You have given Your life for me so that I can have real life now.

In Your class, Lord, everyone receives an A, not because of their achievement but because of the work their Teacher has done for them.

Social Time

Serve simple refreshments and have a time for conversation and mingling.

ADDITIONAL PROGRAM IDEAS

For another "get-acquainted game," mark one side of the room A and the other side B. Ask persons to listen carefully to the A and B choices on the list below. If their choice is A, they are to walk to the side of the room which is marked A. If their choice is B, they are to walk to the side of the room marked B. Give people a chance to notice where others are standing in the room. Parents can choose according to how they felt when they were in junior high school, not how they want their children to feel. The youth will choose according to their current feelings.

I would rather:

A. Get an A in an easy course, or B. Get a B in a hard course.

A. Be the teacher's favorite, or B. Be the class's favorite.

A. Eat the cafeteria food, or B. Carry my lunch.

A. Go to the nurse when I feel sick, or B. Tough it out myself.

A. Walk to school, or B. Ride the school bus.

A. Be known as a good athlete, or B. Be known as a good student.

A. Take all tough courses, or B. Take all easy courses.

A. Get sent to the principal, or B. Have to stand in the corner.

A. Have my parents meet my teachers, or B. Never have my parents meet my teachers.

A. Spend all day in gym class, or B. Spend all day in math class.

A. Kiss the cutest kid in the class, or B. Be the cutest kid in the class.

A. Help the homeroom teacher after school, or B. Go right home after school.

A. Go on a field trip to a museum, or B. Go on a field trip to a factory.

A. Find out I have the highest IQ in the class, or B. Not know my IQ.

A. Get a good mark by cheating, or B. Flunk and remain honest.

A. Have the teacher grade my paper, or B. Have my parents grade my paper.

A. Have a male teacher, or B. Have a female teacher.

A. Do my homework right away, or B. Let homework go till the last minute.

A. Do more than enough for a teacher I like, or B. Just do enough to get by even though I like the teacher.

A. Be pretty good in *most* things, or B. Be extremely good in a *few* things.

You may change any of these selections or add to them. A game like this can be lots of fun and can be an "eye opener" to family members.

Lillian (Biviano) Barron is a free-lance curriculum writer and a local church Christian educator in Carnegie, Pennsylvania. She has been a director of Christian education and a director of youth ministries. Ms. Barron has also been a youth conference leader and a workshop leader in Christian education.

RELATIONSHIPS
RELATIONSHIPS
RELATIONSHIPS

RELATIONSHIPS

RELATIONSHIPS

getting what you want

IDENTIFYING AND GETTING WHAT YOU WANT FROM RELATIONSHIPS

David Y. Hirano
Peter M. Hirano

GOALS

The goals for this program are to identify what junior highers want from relationships and to experience two ways of getting what is wanted.

WHY?

We all want various things from relationships with other people. Often we make people guess what we want. In addition, some junior highers often cannot say what they want. In human relationships, wants and needs must be verbalized, or at least made clear, in order to have them filled by other people. In this program, the junior highers will consider what they want from relationships. Since the peer relationship is very important, this program will provide opportunities for the young people to test out some things with peers.

Christians are told to love one another (Matthew 22:34-40), but we don't talk about which behavior is loving. This program helps junior highers become very specific about actions which are desirable from (and for) friends.

The leader will serve best as a facilitator and enabler. During the exercises, the junior higher may need some suggestions from the leader (some of them are listed in the directions for each step). The leader may make suggestions but must also be careful to give freedom to the junior higher to make his or her own choices.

The adult leader will be most effective when he or she models what a friend is by giving himself or herself, by listening, and by giving feedback.

PREPARATION

Items needed:
1. Newsprint and felt-tipped pens or a chalkboard, chalk, and eraser
2. Paper
3. A pencil for each participant
4. A die (singular for "dice")
5. 15 or more 3″ x 5″ cards on which are written questions about faith, relationships, hobbies, etc. Each card contains one question. Sample questions are "What characteristic do you like most in your best friend?" "If you and your friend were lost, what would you want most from him or her?" "What does church mean to you?" "What is your favorite subject in school and why do you like it?" "What do you like most about your family?" Other questions may be gathered from junior highers prior to the program, or the leader may dream them up.
6. A hat, box, or something to hold the cards.

PROCEDURE

Getting Started

Begin by singing one or more songs and/or having the business session (i.e., making announcements, etc.). MAKE SURE THAT NEWCOMERS ARE INTRODUCED TO THE GROUP!!

Introduce the Topic

Comment, "All of us want friends, and from our friends we want certain things. Tonight we will find out what these things are and try some ways to get what we want from our relationships."

Data Collection

Give to each participant a piece of paper and pencil.

For five minutes have each participant jot down as many phrases or words as possible that finish the sentence "I want from my friends. . . ." The leader may want to make some suggestions like "someone to talk to," "someone to play with me," "someone to care for me," "someone not to laugh at me," etc.

After five minutes have each participant share and consolidate his or her list with one other person. After five more minutes, have each pair share and consolidate their list with another pair.

After five more minutes the leader will ask each group of four for its list and will record the items on a piece of newsprint or on the chalkboard. When this is accomplished, the leader and the group may identify the items which are mentioned most often.

WHY?

This exercise is designed to get each person involved. It is important that each person's wants are recorded in some fashion. It is also designed to get junior highers talking to one another.

An Exercise in Giving

Give each person another piece of paper. Say to the group something like, "Choose one person in the group." (If the participants are hesitant, the leader may number off the participants and match them accordingly.) After each person has been paired with another, then give the next direction: "Each of you has a piece of paper; do something with it and give it to your partner." (In this exercise there may be a person without a partner; the leader may want to join this person or may have the person join an existing pair. Junior highers may have difficulty in thinking about what they can do with the piece of paper. The leader may make suggestions like, "draw a picture," "make a flower," "write a short autobiography or poem," "make an airplane," etc.)

Once the exercise has been completed (it should take no more than ten minutes), let the members of the group share what they felt and why they felt that way.

WHY?

This exercise demonstrates that each person has something to give to someone else, even if it is a blank sheet of paper. Building relationships involves the risk of giving. Sometimes gifts are accepted, sometimes rejected; but someone has to give something before a relationship can start.

Play a Game

Divide the group into two equal groups (if unequal, the leader can play).

One group becomes the inner circle facing outward, the other becomes the outer group facing inward. There should be an equal number face to face.

The leader throws the die, reads the number, and the outer circle moves that number of persons to the right (if the leader calls five, the outer group moves five persons to the right). The leader picks one of the 3″ x 5″ cards from the box or hat and reads the question. Each person on the outer circle answers the question and gives his or her answer to the person facing him or her. The person on the inner circle responds with what he or she has heard. The leader again casts the die; this time the inner group moves the number called, the persons on the inner circle answer the question, and the outer circle listens and feeds back. This is done repeatedly with the outer and inner groups alternating until all have had a chance to speak or to listen to at least five people. Do more if the game is going well.

At the conclusion of the game, the leader may have the group join together and share their feelings and thoughts, then make some concluding remarks.

WHY?

Junior highers need to learn the art of listening and sharing if they are going to get what they want from one another.

Worship

Have someone read Matthew 7:12; 22:34-40.

These verses are the Golden Rule and the Great Commandment. Both are, in Jesus' words, the fulfillment of "the law and the prophets." Following these commandments helps one have satisfying relationships with others, feel good about oneself, and be a good Christian as well.

Conclude with a prayer: "Lord, help us to give, to listen, to risk, and to learn so that we can have friends and be friends, too. In Jesus' name. Amen."

Rev. Dr. David Y. Hirano is the minister of the Nuuanu Congregational Church in Honolulu, Hawaii. Peter M. Hirano is his son, a junior high student at Punahou School in Honolulu, Hawaii.

RELATIONSHIPS

magic broom—or I'm in, you're out

DEALING WITH CLIQUES Marcia J. Patton

GOAL

To explore how we deal with cliques and people who seem stuck-up.

WHY?

One of the problems junior highs face is their relationships to their peers. "Being a part of a group" is especially important. Groups can be good or bad, depending on how they function. Cliques tend to shut out other people, which can easily cause hurt feelings. This program will simulate a "special" or "in" group and give young people a chance to discuss their feelings about this group in the light of the Christian message about love.

PROCEDURE

Introduction

Step 1

Share the goal statement with the group.

Step 2

Read Luke 5:27-32 to the group from a good, readable, and understandable translation. Review the story with the group. Identify the persons and groups in the story. Identify what clique(s) exists in the story.

Play the Game

Step 1

Play a game with a "trick" to it. Instructions for two games follow.

"Scissors" The process of this game is to pass a pair of scissors around the group which is seated in a circle. As a person receives the scissors, he or she says one of two statements: "I received the scissors crossed," or "I received the scissors uncrossed." As each one passes the scissors, he or she says, "I pass the scissors crossed," or "I pass the scissors uncrossed," as the case may be. The "trick" is that the "crossed" or "uncrossed" has nothing to do with the scissors (you can pass them opened or closed). It depends upon whether the person receiving or passing has his or her legs crossed or not.

"Magic Broom" Two people who know the trick are needed for this game: the leader and one other person who will leave the room. The group is seated in a circle. The leader takes a "magic broom," stands in the center, twirls it around twice, and bangs the top of the broom on the floor. After a few seconds the other person leaves the room. After the person has left, the broom begins to "travel" (in the hands of the leader) to a person in the group. After everyone notes to whom the broom "traveled," the leader (still holding the broom) calls back the person who left the room. The person who left then takes the broom. The broom will "travel" (in the hands of the person who left) to the same person again. The "trick" is that the first person in the room to speak after the broom has been banged on the floor is the person to whom the broom will "travel." (This happens *before* the other person leaves the room.)

Only a small group of people should know how to play whichever game you choose. If no one but those conducting the game knows how to play, that is fine. Others in the group may guess the "trick" as the game goes on. That's okay. Guesses should be shared only with those who already know the trick.

Step 2

Stop the game after approximately ten minutes.

WHY?

The reason for setting up this game is to establish an "in" group, the "clique" who knows how the game is played. The others are the outsiders. As a leader, listen to the conversation that takes place within the outside group and between the "outside" and "in" groups.

Reflect upon the Game

Step 1

Give each person a pencil and piece of paper. Ask the group members to write down the following:

A. A color that describes how they feel right now.

B. As many details as possible of the last two minutes of play. (Have a specific event in mind with which they can begin. For example, you could say, "Write down everything you can remember after Jane said, 'I've got it!'")

C. How they think (or know) those in the "in" group felt.

D. How they think (or know) those "outside" felt.

Step 2

Share the responses to the questions in small groups. It would be helpful to have an adult in each small group to facilitate the discussions. Check out the descriptions. What did some people remember that others did not? What were the events that everyone remembered? What were the important happenings? Did the guesses about the feelings come close to the real thing? How do we assume others feel who are not a part of our group?

Step 3

Have the small groups bring a report of their discussions to the total group. Share the reports. Were there any feelings expressed that were a surprise? What does the discussion say about the groups to whom we as individuals relate? What does it say about us as a Christian group?

WHY?

Part of the difficulty of cliques is the feelings that exist on both sides. This exercise is designed to encourage us to talk about those feelings. The questions and responses should lead to statements of how we relate to groups in daily life.

Celebration

Step 1

Have each person share with the group two things he or she likes about the group. This can be done verbally, listed on newsprint, or shared with one other person and then the whole group.

Step 2

Have a circle prayer, or stand in a circle and sing "We Are One in the Spirit."

ADDITIONAL PROGRAM IDEAS

An Alternate Way to Share the Scripture

Step 1

Divide the group into tax collectors, outcasts, disciples, and Pharisees.

Step 2

Tell the story in Luke 5:27-32, paraphrasing, adding details to the story, and stretching it out in order to create a meaningful experience. Whoever tells the story should know it well. While the story is being told, have each person write down how he or she is feeling as the person he or she is in the story.

Step 3: Reflection

Have each group of "persons" share their "feelings" (what they wrote down) with the group.

Step 4

A discussion may then follow along this line:

"Who were the outsiders in this story?"

"How does an outcast feel?"

"How does a person that is in an 'in' group feel?"

"How can an 'in' group and a stranger be reconciled?"

"What does this say about what our actions should be as Christians?"

"What Scriptures do we know that support what we think?" (See Matthew 7:12; 22:34-40; Luke 10:25-37.)

"How can we deal with strangers in our midst?"

Up Is Down

This is a short film available from Mass Media Associates (Mass Media Associates, 2116 N. Charles Street, Baltimore, MD 21218); it can be used as part of the introduction or as part of the celebration.

The Man Who Had to Sing, Everyday Chronicle, and *The Fifth One,* other short films also available from Mass Media Associates, can be used as part of the introduction or celebration. They can also be used with some reflection, as was suggested with the Scripture.

Why Am I Afraid to Tell You Who I Am?

For further study of this area try this book and filmstrip, available from Argus Communications, 7440 Natchez Avenue, Niles, IL 60648.

Marcia J. Patton is minister of Christian education and youth of the First Baptist Church, Salt Lake City, Utah.

RELATIONSHIPS

how would you pick a date?

SHARING WHAT INFLUENCES THE CHOICE OF A DATE   Rosemary Oaks-Lee

GOAL

To provide junior highs with an opportunity to express and hear what influences the choice of a date.

WHY?

Junior highs are being thrust into the adult world; and although they are usually spectators, they become increasingly concerned about who or what they should become. Unfortunately, in our society most of our information about what we are supposed to be and how we are supposed to act comes from the media, peers of the same sex, and older people's jokes rather than from peers of the other sex—who are, for most of us, the very ones whose favor we seek.

This exercise is designed to give junior highs some information about what others might look for in a date and to give youth some practice in sharing those expectations.

Note: The term "other sex" is used intentionally throughout these instructions. In relationships between males and females, it is important to remember that we are more similar (in feelings, needs, hopes, values) than different—and by no means *opposite*.

PREPARATION

Materials: paper or 3″ x 5″ cards
            pencils
            newsprint, markers, and tape, or chalkboard and chalk

PROCEDURE

Step 1

Explain that you will read a question, then two responses. One corner of the room represents the first response, another corner the second. As you read each question, each youth should respond by going to the corner that indicates his or her choice. Do not ask anyone to explain his or her choice. Allow enough time for each to make a choice and see how others choose; then read the next question. Do not allow discussion yet. (3-4 minutes)

Note: You should explain that there are no right or wrong responses and that each should respond as he or she feels right now, even though he or she might feel differently tomorrow. No "fence-sitting," please! Try to answer. Some suggestions for questions follow.

1. Which is your favorite holiday—*Easter* or *Christmas?*
2. Would you rather be a *skunk* or a *hippo?*
3. Would you rather go to the movies with *one other person* or *a group of kids?*
4. Would you rather play softball with someone of the *same sex* or someone of the *other sex*?
5. Would you rather be the *Ping Pong ball* or the *Ping Pong paddle?*
6. Would you rather have a serious discussion with someone of the *same sex* or someone of the *other sex?*
7. Would you rather prepare supper with someone of the *same sex* or someone of the *other sex?*
8. Would you rather take your vacation at the *seashore* or in the *mountains?*
9. Would you rather tell a secret to someone of the *same sex* or someone of the *other sex?*
10. Would you rather *love someone else* or *be loved by someone?*

Step 2

Have each individually think about his or her class at school and choose five people from it with whom he or she would most like to "go out." Do not identify the people aloud. On paper have each person list what it is about these people that made him or her choose them (no names needed). (There may be several things about one and few about others.) Out of those characteristics listed, have each choose the *five* that are most important to him or her. Rank them in order of importance. (5-10 minutes)

Step 3

Choose a partner of the same sex. Each pair shares those five characteristics (and the others, if you wish). Together make a new list of the three most important characteristics of a date. (5 minutes)

Step 4

Join with one (or two) other pair(s) of the same sex; again make a list of the five most important characteristics. When this list is complete, each group should record its list on newsprint or chalkboard. Identify whether the group is male or female. (10-15 minutes)
Note: You may vary the size of the groups in Steps 3 and 4 depending on the size of your group. Step 3 groups could include two to three persons; Step 4 groups could include four to six persons.

Step 5: Fishbowl

After everyone has had a chance to read the lists, ask the boys to sit in a group with the girls in a circle around them. Ask the boys to discuss: How do you feel about the list the girls made? How did you feel when you read it? Do you fit the things listed? If so, how do you feel? If not, what are your feelings? (5-7 minutes)
Reverse the fishbowl so that the girls are in the center responding to the list the boys made. (5-7 minutes)

If there is time after the fishbowl, you may wish to ask the group to discuss: "Would you have said different things if we had been talking about a *friend* instead of a *date?* If this had not been a coed group?" "What things might keep you from dating people who have the characteristics you named?"

Step 6

With the entire group together, talk about the exercise, perhaps by completing these sentences:
While we were making the lists, I felt. . . .
While the (boys, girls) were in the fishbowl, I felt. . . .
From this program I learned. . . .
For me, the most difficult thing about this exercise was. . . .
For me, the easiest thing about this exercise was. . . .
(5-10 minutes)

ADDITIONAL PROGRAM IDEA

The following idea could be used between Steps 5 and 6.
Ask the youth to help you define a situation which volunteers will role-play. Some possible suggestions are:
—What is a difficult situation in dating or in asking for a date?
—A girl invites a boy; a boy invites a girl.
—Refuse an invitation of someone with whom you do not want to go out.
—Refuse an invitation because you are waiting for someone else to ask.
After each role play, invite the actors to talk about what they felt in doing their roles; then ask the entire group to reflect on what it saw happening. Discuss alternative ways of acting and reacting.

Rosemary Oaks-Lee is adviser for the York churches' senior high youth group in York, New York. She is also the training and education assistant for the Genesee Region Family Planning Program in Rochester, New York, and is a free-lance sexuality educator.

RELATIONSHIPS

when you fight with your parents

IDENTIFYING AND MINIMIZING CONFLICTS WITH PARENTS　　　Elizabeth J. Loughhead

---

GOALS

To help junior high young people identify areas of conflict with their parents. To consider how these conflicts arise and junior highs' responsibility in the creation of them. To explore possible ways of minimizing such conflicts. To discover if the Christian gospel speaks to the problem of fighting with parents and the resolution of the conflicts.

WHY?

Junior high youth are moving rapidly from childhood to adulthood, but their feelings and emotions are ambivalent. Almost simultaneously they want to be independent and dependent. At one moment they want the freedom to make their own decisions, and at the next moment they want the security of being told what to do. They wish the privileges of the adult world without assuming the required responsibilities. Communication between youth and parents tends to break down as the young people rebel against what have been the rules and practices of the family, while demanding the right to manage their own lives. Parents feel their authority threatened, become unsure in their parenting role, and see only chaos ahead for their children. The youth are confused about their feelings, the reaction of their parents, and the atmosphere of conflict which surrounds them so frequently.

PREPARATION

The materials needed for this program are minimal and can be gathered quickly from home or a church school classroom. Alternative materials will be suggested which can be used at points in the program to make it more interesting but which are not necessary to the success of the program.

Materials: paper and pencils, large sheets of newsprint or a chalkboard, chalk, crayons, colored paper, and scissors.

Optional materials: two sets of Tinker Toys, backpack or sturdy box, heavy stones, bricks, or blocks.

The opening questionnaire can be written on a large sheet of newsprint or a chalkboard, but it would be easier to use if it were mimeographed or duplicated in some way.

PROCEDURE

Questionnaire

As the young people arrive, have each one answer the questions as privately as possible, filling out the mimeographed sheet or using paper and pencil to answer questions on the chalkboard or newsprint.

1. I had my last argument with one of my parents _____ .
2. It was about _____ .
3. My parents and I agree the most about ___ _____ .
4. My parents and I disagree the most about _____ .
5. I fight more often with my mom about ___ _____ .
6. I fight more often with my dad about ____ _____ .
7. I think the time I come in at night should be decided by _____ .

8. I think when and what I study should be decided by _____ .
9. I think that _____ should decide when a person is old enough to start dating.
10. I think that the use of the family phone should be decided by _____ .
11. I think _____ should decide when I can go out on a school night and what activities are appropriate for a school night.
12. I think that the clothes I wear should be decided by _____ .

The leaders may add other questions which they know to be appropriate for their group. The questionnaires may be used during the rest of the program. It might be interesting to use the same questions again after several weeks to determine if change has been made in any area(s) of conflict.

Further Identify the Areas of Conflict

As the junior highs answer the questionnaire, the leader posts on the walls around the room sheets of paper, each with an area of parent-youth conflict lettered on it. Areas of conflict such as GRADES, HOMEWORK, CLOTHES, PHONE USE, MONEY, DATING, HOURS, FRIENDS, RULES OF CONDUCT, etc., should be used. At each sheet have three crayons: red for indicating that this is an area of major conflict, blue for an area of minor concern, yellow for showing that this is an area over which she or he and parents never fight. When a young person finishes answering the questionnaire, have him or her go from sheet to sheet and register an opinion concerning the area of conflict. The group members may then see which topics are of greatest concern for them. The leader should give an opportunity for the young people to add other topics not listed.

Small Group Discussion

The group should be divided into small groups of three or four. Each group should choose or be assigned a topic which has been determined to be an area of major conflict. Ask each group to discuss:
1. When does this become a conflict situation?
2. Who creates the conflict?
3. Does this have to be an area of conflict?
4. Do John 13:34-35 and 1 Corinthians 13:5 have anything to say about this conflict?

The groups may report back to the total group; but if time is short, the discussion in the small groups is "first priority."

Exercise in Communication

Have members of the group sit in pairs with the partners' backs to each other. Each person should have paper and crayons or colored paper and scissors. If sets of Tinkertoys are available, use two members of the group at a time, each with a set of Tinkertoys. The leader calls out a subject, such as airplane, automobile, or engine. The individuals create their own version of the subject without looking at the other person's. When both are finished, the pictures or objects are compared. Although the announced subject was the same, the finished products will be quite different.

WHY?

Many conflicts between parents and youth arise because the picture in the parent's head is very different from the picture in the young person's head. For example, Mother says, "Don't be late." The picture in her head is 8:30 P.M., while the picture in the head of her daughter is some time before midnight. Dad may tell his son, "When your studying is finished, you may go over to Debbie's house." The picture in the father's head is of every assignment done with A-quality work and any possible extra credit completed. The picture in the son's head may be that of one assignment finished, some reading skimmed, and some work left for a better time. The exercise of creating pictures or objects which differ even though the topic is the same is to help the young people see how problems develop unless clear communication is practiced.

The group members should list on newsprint or chalkboard as many different meanings as possible for the following commands:

Don't be late!
Wear something appropriate!
Do your homework!
Be careful with your money!

They should spend some time discussing whose responsibility it is to find out what is meant by a request or rule made by a parent, how they can reasonably express their opinions, and how conflicts can be avoided by the simple procedure of understanding expectations and working out differences ahead of time.

Closing

Each young person should find a spot where she or he can sit comfortably and alone but within earshot of the leader.

The leader asks each person to think of the last argument or the most recent big fight the youth had with her or his parents, and then to consider these questions:

1. What was the fight about?
2. Was it really worth all the emotional upheaval?
3. What went wrong?
4. Could the fight have been avoided?
5. What could I have done to make the situation better?
6. What would that love of which the Bible speaks have me do when I disagree with my parents?
7. Can I ask God to help me to be a peacemaker in my own family?
8. What can I try to do for this next week that will help reduce conflicts between me and my parents?

If the mood is right, the leader or a youth may close with a spoken prayer.

ADDITIONAL PROGRAM IDEAS

Solving Problems of Conflict

Present to the group members some conflicts between a young person and the parents. Let them brainstorm some solutions to the problem. See if they can come up with creative ways for avoiding the conflict in the future.

EXAMPLE: The young person has a reasonable curfew but cannot seem to get in on time. The parents resent staying awake to be sure their child is safely in.

CREATIVE SOLUTION: The young person sets an alarm for the time he or she must be in and assumes the responsibility for arriving home in time to turn off the alarm before it awakens the parents. The parents can relax and go to sleep, and the burden of responsibility is placed upon the youth.

EXAMPLE: A junior high youth breaks a trust and lies to his/her parents about it.

CREATIVE SOLUTION: The youth names the punishment and proves to the parents that she or he realizes that renewed trust must be built up all over again.

EXAMPLE: Continuous conflict is present in a family because of the clothing choices of the young person.

CREATIVE SOLUTION: The youth agrees to earn or save a portion of the cost of the clothing and to wear what will please the parents when going out with them to church or other places, while being allowed to wear items of his or her choosing for recreation or times with peers.

Recognizing Pressures

Pressures upon individuals can often create or magnify conflicts. This exercise can help people feel in their own bodies the pressures and burdens experienced by others and thus can help them become more understanding.

First, have one person represent youth and either wear a backpack or hold a sturdy box. Others in the group drop a heavy object into the pack or box while naming a pressure youth experience. Examples: getting good grades, being popular, making the team, earning money for college, wearing the right clothes, and so forth.

Second, have a person represent a parent and wear the pack or hold the box while others drop in heavy objects representing the pressures a mother or father might feel. Examples: earning enough to feed and clothe the family, keeping a clean house, satisfying the boss, working responsibly in the community, providing the luxuries the family would like, holding an office at church, helping children be a credit to the family, being a good wife or husband, and so on.

WHY?

Youth are very aware of the pressures they face and may feel that parents, teachers, coaches, and peers are all "laying something on them." This exercise is designed to help them realize that adults face many pressures, also, and that they need compassion and understanding, too.

For Intergenerational Use

The topic of conflict with parents is a natural for an intergenerational program. The suggestions in this program outline could be used very well in a session where youth and their parents were present. Each of the following suggestions is listed according to which section in the original program it belongs.

Questionnaire: Parents could answer the questionnaire, also.

Further Identify the Areas of Conflict:
    Parents could identify areas of conflict but

use crayons of different colors.

Small Group Discussion:

Small group discussion should be included in the program, but youth might feel freer to discuss in a group composed of their peers. Final sharing could be done with the total group.

Exercise in Communication:

The exercise in communication is very good for youth and parents to do together so they will recognize the necessity for clear communication.

Closing:

The closing is appropriate for both parents and youth since when there is a conflict, it involves both generations.

The additional activities are also especially good for an intergenerational event. For the Solving Problems of Conflict activity, let the parents pose a problem and the youth develop creative ways to solve it, and then reverse the process. In the Recognizing Pressures exercise, a parent should take the role of the youth and feel the pressures dropped upon him or her by the youth. Then a youth should become a parent and feel the heavy burdens laid upon him or her by the adults.

Elizabeth J. Loughhead, a graduate of Colgate-Rochester Divinity School and a former president of the Board of Educational Ministries of the American Baptist Churches in the U.S.A., is also a mother of three and a member of Calvary Baptist Church, Denver, Colorado, where she has been a church school teacher of junior highs for eleven years.

RELATIONSHIPS

ouch!

EXPLORING WAYS WE EXCLUDE AND INCLUDE OTHERS   **Terry Sue Fischer**

GOALS

To create an awareness of how things we say influence the way others feel. To put that awareness into practice with an activity.

WHY?

People of junior high age (and older) have a tendency to use a lot of "put-downs" or insults. These often happen as a part of good times with several friends which either purposefully or accidentally exclude others. It is important for them to become aware of how they are excluding others and how others feel as a result of this experience. Somewhat related to that behavior is the fact that junior-high-aged people need to be challenged and to experience adventure in order to feel good about themselves. This exercise is designed to encourage sensitivity to others' feelings and a sense of self-satisfaction that comes from creating something fun and useful. Our feelings about ourselves and others are interrelated. It is hoped that the primary session and the additional program helps outlined below will enrich each other.

PREPARATION

Cartoon, short game. The cartoon provided in this program must be drawn on newsprint or the chalkboard ahead of time.

PROCEDURE

Activity 1 (10 to 15 minutes)

Start with a game which your group would enjoy. "Elbow Tag" or "The Boiler Burst" would do well. "Elbow Tag" is an indoor or outdoor game where the group members pair off and each pair links elbows. They scatter around an area. There is also a runner and a chaser. When the runner gets tired of running around the pairs or is about to be caught, she or he can link elbows with one person in a pair. Then the person on the other end of the pair (which is now a group of three) has to run and try to avoid being caught by the chaser. If the runner gets caught, he or she turns and chases the chaser. (The chaser becomes the runner; and therefore, he or she has the privilege of linking elbows.) This is a no-win, no-lose game, and everyone should have a chance to play each position. The leader ends the game whenever he or she desires.

In "The Boiler Burst," the youth each take a seat in a circle of chairs. One person stands in the middle to begin the game. There should be only enough chairs for those who are sitting. The person in the middle begins inventing a story to tell the group. When she or he says, "The boiler burst," everyone has to change places (at least two seats away) and the storyteller tries to get a seat. The person left standing begins another story. This game, too, continues until someone purposely ends it.

Activity 2 (5 to 10 minutes)

After the game, show the cartoon strip. Facilitate discussion. Do you think Elmer George really believes what he says? Why or why not? Briefly talk about things we do that hurt one another.

Activity 3 (10 to 15 minutes)

Divide into groups of four to seven persons, depending on the size of your group, with a leader for each group. Tell the youth that you are going to play a game, a different kind of game, one that may cause

45

them some frustration (or you may identify this as a role play). Then ask one person in each group to leave the room. Instruct them (in private) to try to become a part of the groups. Instruct the groups (without the outsiders hearing) that they are going to plan an ice-cream party or whatever. (It's especially useful if they actually are planning a real activity.) They are to try to keep the outsiders out by whatever means they want. Get the discussion started, and invite the outsiders to join the groups. After several minutes of this role play (use your intuition), have the outsiders move out of hearing, and instruct the groups to begin to include these persons when they return. Then have the outsiders return and role-play accordingly. After a few minutes, discuss the experience. (How did the people in the groups feel? How did the persons left out feel? Are there times in real life when we behave like we just did? At home, at school, at church?)

Closure

Close by sharing in the reading of James 3:3-10 or other appropriate Scripture, such as John 13:34-35.

ADDITIONAL PROGRAM IDEAS

This is an alternative to Activity 1. This is a little more forceful and a little more risky. Tell the youth they are going to play a game, and then divide them into groups of five. After they are in groups of five, change your mind; tell them you've decided groups of four will be better, and ask them to eliminate one person in each group by some process. Play a short game (any game for four). After the game, get the total group together and help them share their feelings about the experience of eliminating one person from the group. (How did you feel when I said we would play a game? How did you feel when I said you had to eliminate someone? How did the people remaining in the group and the people left out feel? Are there real-life situations which compare to the activity we just did? At home, at school, at church?)

An additional activity which can be done after Activity 2 is to encourage each youth to make his or her own cartoon sequence about a time when he or she has been hurt by something someone said or did to him or her.

Terry Sue McGee Fischer was formerly Christian education coordinator at the First Baptist Church, McMinnville, Oregon.

DECISIONS
DECISIONS
DECISIONS

DECISIONS

DECISIONS

about me

UNDERSTANDING SEXUAL DEVELOPMENT AND DECISIONS　　　　**Rosemary Oakes-Lee**

GOALS

To help junior highs name some of the changes taking place in their lives, especially those relating to developing sexuality, and to hear about changes in the lives of their peers. To clarify some of the feelings about those changes and some of the decisions relating to these feelings which may be facing individual youth.

WHY?

This is a time of many changes for youth, especially physical changes and the new emotions which go with them. Decisions are being made about those changes, sometimes with little or no thought about the consequences. Often the changes are very personal and happen without a context. Youth do not have a chance to talk about them or to learn that others feel similarly (as well as differently). Just talking about what is happening to us and "naming it" and hearing others "name it" help us to understand it better. The first step of good decision making is facing what our situation is and what alternatives might be open to us and how we feel about them.

If junior high youth find an open and understanding atmosphere in the church, perhaps they will be more willing to consider Christian values in these decisions.

Note: These activities may be most helpful to your youth if members of both sexes are involved, but they can be used successfully with all-male or all-female groups.

PREPARATION

On a piece of newsprint or a chalkboard write the sentences to be completed in the closing section ("I learned that I . . . ," etc.).

Materials:　paper or 3″ x 5″ cards
　　　　　　pencils
　　　　　　newsprint, markers, and tape, or chalk-board and chalk

PROCEDURE

Note: Adult advisers should feel free to participate in each of the following activities. Youth like to hear adults' responses to these concerns, and it will help them to feel comfortable talking about themselves if you are willing to share about yourself. (There is a difference, though, between sharing your own feelings and experiences and "preaching" at them.)

It should be explained that anyone has a right to "pass" if he or she does not want to share. (If you find, however, that a large number of your group choose not to participate, you may wish to interrupt the exercise and say, "I notice many of you have not participated. How are you feeling about this exercise?" or "What are some of the reasons people have chosen to pass?" Even in this discussion, a participant should still be allowed to pass.)

Step 1

Ask the youth to complete each of the sentences below as you read them aloud. Have them share their responses, using *one* of the following processes:

—As sentences are read, have them write their responses on paper or a 3″ x 5″ card. (No names, please.) Pass the papers to the leader, who shuffles them and hands them out again (unidentified). Each person reads the responses on the paper he or she has been given. (15-20 minutes)

—Have all group members lie on their backs on the floor. As each sentence is read aloud, each person responds aloud to the entire group. (15 minutes)

—Each person writes his or her responses on paper, then chooses a partner with whom he or she shares the first one. Choose another partner; share the second, etc. (15 minutes)

WHY?

Some groups are used to sharing fairly personally with each other. Other junior highs will find it easier to share if they have a chance to *write* a response first or if they do not have to identify it as their own.

Sentences to be completed

1. One of the things that bugs me about being (your age) is. . . .
2. One of the things that I like about being (your age) is. . . .
3. One of the things I wonder about getting older is. . . .
4. For me, one of the hardest decisions is. . . .
5. In the last two years, the biggest change in me has been. . . .
6. In the next three years, the way I expect I will change most is. . . .
7. One thing about sex I'd like to know more about is. . . .
8. If my parents talked with me about sex, I would feel. . . .

Step 2

On paper or 3″ x 5″ cards, have each person write three things he or she likes about himself or herself and three things he or she dislikes about himself or herself. Encourage the youth to spread out and work separately. Then have each person share his or her likes and dislikes as one or two group members record them on newsprint or a chalkboard under the headings "Things I Like About Me" and "Things I Don't Like About Me." (5 minutes)

Step 3

Encourage the youth to talk about the lists, asking questions such as: "What do you notice when you look at the lists? Which of the dislikes can you change? How? Which things cannot be changed (must be accepted)?" (5-10 minutes)

Step 4

Put up the newsprint with the following incomplete sentences:
"I learned that I. . . ."
"I was surprised that I. . . ."
"I was glad that I. . . ."
"I was disappointed that I. . . ."
Ask each person to complete aloud or in writing one or more of the above sentences, referring to the experiences of the session. Explain that no one, including yourself or other leaders, is to respond to anyone's contribution. When someone completes a sentence, nod or say, "Thank you," in acknowledgment. (3-5 minutes)

ADDITIONAL PROGRAM IDEAS

For junior highs, many of the changes they experience and decisions they face revolve around issues of sexuality. A longer program is needed to deal with those concerns in any depth. In order to talk about the things they want and need to know, adolescents need a climate of "unshockableness"; of freedom to hold their own views; of leadership whom they have tested and found to be knowledgeable, comfortable, willing to share or listen, accepting of what they fear may be "silly" concerns, and nonjudgmental of how they make decisions.

Few of us were exposed to such open learning experiences about sexuality. We have not had good models to copy. We have not been encouraged to examine openly our own attitudes and values. How can we facilitate in such a process for others? It is important that anyone who hopes to teach human sexuality programs prepares by seeking appropriate training and self-assessment. Information about such training programs is available through your local family planning or family-service agencies, nearby colleges, or denominational family-life departments. (The Unitarian church has developed training and a program for junior highs which this author highly recommends.)

RESOURCES

Here are a few of the resources with which you may wish to become familiar to help your group explore further some of the questions or issues raised:

Books

Pomeroy, Wardell B., *Boys and Sex*. New York: Delacorte Press, imprint of The Dial Press, 1968.

_____, *Girls and Sex*. New York: Delacorte Press, imprint of The Dial Press, 1969.

Morrison, Eleanor; and Price, Mila Underhill, *Values in Sexuality: A New Approach to Sex Education*. New York: Hart Publishing Co., Inc., 1974.

Other Resources

Rocky Mountain Planned Parenthood has published several delightful pamphlets about puberty, responsible sexuality, and male-female roles. Write for its publication list to:

Rocky Mountain Planned Parenthood Publications
1852 Vine Street
Denver, CO 80206

Your local planned parenthood or family-planning agency has staff and resources available to help you respond to your youth's questions about sexuality.

Rosemary Oaks-Lee is adviser for the York churches' senior high youth group in York, New York. She is also Training and Education Assistant for the Genesee Region Family Planning Program in Rochester, New York, and is a free-lance sexuality educator.

DECISIONS

when is honesty the best policy?

SHARING STANDARDS FOR HONESTY INTERGENERATIONALLY   Thomas G. Bayes, Jr., Terry J. Ging

Christians are taught to speak the truth in love and to be honest and fair in their dealings with others. We are taught to respect our fellow human beings, as they are also created by God in God's image and because God loves them, also. One of the problems which teenagers have with the idea that they must practice total honesty is that many adults around them—sometimes even their parents and teachers—live by a double standard. They may not always require the same behavior of themselves that they seem to require of teenagers.

Here is a series of exercises focusing on issues related to honesty for junior highs, their parents, and siblings who are first graders or older. It could be presented as an evening program, as part of an intergenerational series, or as the educational content for a family retreat weekend.

GOALS

To help junior highs and their family members clarify their feelings about honesty. To help family members discover the standards for honesty which exist within their family, including whether or not there is a double standard between the values which individuals hold for themselves and those which they hold for other members of their families.

PROCEDURE

Icebreaker: "Personality Bingo" Game (10-15 minutes)

Purpose
To get people talking to one another.
Materials
One pencil and one "Personality Bingo" sheet for each participant.

Instructions
Find someone who has the characteristic described in each square. Have that person sign his/her name in that square. When you have completed four squares across, down, or diagonally, yell, "Bingo!" (P.S.—You cannot sign your own sheet!)

Someone who has the same color eyes you do.	Someone who likes to go camping.	Someone who owns a yellow bicycle.	Someone who has never been in the hospital.
Someone whose birthday is in the same month as yours.	Someone who wears glasses.	Someone who hates strawberry ice cream.	Someone who tells you a joke.
Someone who is left-handed.	Someone who is wearing sneakers.	Someone who won't walk under ladders.	The person in the room you have known the longest (other than someone in your family).
Someone whose favorite sport is hockey.	The first person you spoke to when you arrived (other than family).	Someone who loves to play games.	Someone you've never met before.

As people arrive for the session, pass out bingo sheets and pencils. Younger children may need to work with someone older.

When someone declares a bingo, read aloud the characteristics used to form the bingo and those who signed for these characteristics. Let the game go for ten or fifteen minutes. Several bingos may be declared before the game is halted.

"George Washington and the Cherry Tree" (20-30 minutes)

Purpose

To encourage sharing within families and to help individuals explore the values related to honesty which are at work in a family situation.

Materials

Copies of the story (one for every four or five people) and pencils.

Once upon a time, George Washington, who later became the father of our country, was a little boy. He lived on a plantation in Virginia with his mother, Mrs. Washington, his father, Mr. Washington, his sister, Mary, and his brother, Jonathan.

For his birthday George's parents gave him a shiny new axe so that he could cut some trees for the winter wood pile.

About a week later, Mr. Washington was coming in from the fields when he noticed that the family's only cherry tree, which grew in the backyard, had been chopped to pieces. What Mr. Washington *didn't* know was that _____ had done it.

That night a family council was called. "Well," said Father, "we have a problem. Someone has chopped down the cherry tree."

"What is the best way to find out who did it?" Mother asked.

Jonathan said, "I think the best way to find out who did this is to _____
_____ ."

Mary said, "_____
_____ ."

George said, " _____
_____ ."

Mother said, "I think we ought to _____
_____ ."

Father added, "_____
_____ ."

Finally it was decided that the best way to find out the truth was to _____
_____ .

Then what happened next was _____
_____
_____ .

The moral of the story is: _____
_____ .

Instructions

Divide the group into "simulated families" (small groups which include adults and children, all of whom are not related to one another). Give each group a copy of the George Washington story. Ask the members of the group to complete the story with everyone's help.

After each "family" has completed the story, discuss some of these questions briefly with the total group:

1. In your story, who chopped down the cherry tree?
2. How did the Washingtons decide to discover the truth?
3. Did the truth come out? How?
4. How was the guilty person treated?
5. What was the moral of your story?

Dissolve the "simulated families," and have people return to their natural families for the next game.

Simulation Game: "Truth and Consequences" (45-60 minutes)

On a life-size, three-sided "game board," families move together to various positions, discussing and making decisions about questions of honesty.

Purpose

To provide an opportunity for individuals to compare their values concerning honesty with those of others in the family and to discover whether or not each has double standards for honesty.

Materials

Large sheets of colored paper (three sheets each of seven different colors), twenty-one smaller sheets of white paper, copies of the Answer Blanks Sheet found after the list of twenty-one questions (one for each participant), "street signs" (Adult Drive, etc.), pencils, and chairs (optional).

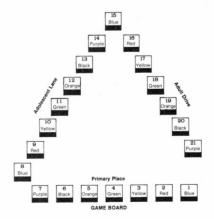

Preparation: Set up the game with twenty-one numbered squares using the color sequence shown in the diagram above. Print the numbers on the colored paper. Post "street signs" (Adult Drive, etc.) to label each of the three sides of the triangle. Write the questions below on the white sheets of paper and attach them to the appropriate numbered square. You may want to place a few chairs near each square so that families can sit during their discussions.

Questions:

1. Your parents have gone out, telling you to practice the piano for an hour while they are gone. Do you quit early?
2. Mike has invited you to his birthday party. You don't want to go. Do you find an excuse for not going?
3. Your next-door neighbor has the ugliest, meanest dog you've ever seen. She asks you if you like the dog. Do you avoid telling the truth?
4. You see someone in your class pull the fire alarm. The teacher asks if anyone knows who did it. Do you keep quiet?
5. You are given enough lunch money for a week, but you eat lunch only twice. Can you use the rest of the money to help buy a birthday present for your sister?
6. You see Joe, the neighborhood pest, coming up the sidewalk. Do you have your brother answer the door and say that you're not feeling well?
7. You and your friend are running through her house. She knocks over the portable TV. You put it back up, but it doesn't work. Do you tell her to act as if nothing has happened?
8. You're taking an exam in school. The teacher has left the room. Your friend, sitting next to you, offers you the answer. Do you take it from him?
9. You're asked to attend a long and boring youth group session. Your homework *could* wait. Do you tell the group that you have to study?
10. You go out on a date with your best friend's favorite cousin. The date is a disaster. Your best friend asks you if you had a good time. Do you avoid the issue?
11. Your youth group is staying overnight in the church. Someone rips the carpet. Unless the guilty party is found, there will be no more overnights. You know who did it. Do you keep it to yourself?
12. Your parents give you $5 and tell you to get your hair cut. You have a friend cut it. Do you keep the money?
13. You promised to work the lights for a school play rehearsal, but you forgot that your church youth group is going skiing at the same time. You really want to go skiing. Do you get someone else to work the lights?
14. You're riding with your friend in his parents' car. He's showing off and accidentally scrapes the car against a post. He plans to tell his parents that that scrape happened while the car was parked. Will you support his story?
15. Your boss is gone for the day, and things are fairly slow. Do you take this opportunity to catch up on some personal correspondence?
16. You're invited to a wedding which is not particularly important to you. You're free, but you don't want to go. Do you tell them that you're busy?
17. Obviously proud, a friend asks your opinion about her son's solo in a recent school concert. You know that he performed poorly. Do you answer with a half-truth?
18. A teenager confides in you that he robbed the house down the street. Do you keep the information confidential?
19. Your employer sends you to a conference and gives you $10 in cash for lunch. You spend only $8.50. Do you keep the remaining $1.50?
20. Your secretary tells you that an angry client is on the phone. You don't want to take the call right now. Do you tell your secretary to say that you're not available?
21. A friend is applying for an important job. The application asks if she has ever been under psychiatric care. She has, briefly, but fears that admitting this would jeopardize the job. Do you advise her to leave the question blank?

ANSWER BLANKS SHEET

PRIMARY PLACE	ADOLESCENT LANE	ADULT DRIVE
1. _____	8. _____	15. _____
2. _____	9. _____	16. _____
3. _____	10. _____	17. _____
4. _____	11. _____	18. _____
5. _____	12. _____	19. _____
6. _____	13. _____	20. _____
7. _____	14. _____	21. _____

Game Procedure

On each side of the game board, questions are directed to a specific age group (e.g., Adolescent Lane questions are directed to teenagers). The members of the family who are in that age group must make their own decisions after receiving advice and opinions from the rest of the family. They write their yes or no decision in the appropriate space on the answer sheet. The other family members write on their sheets what they think the individual should have decided.

Each family does not necessarily cover every square on every side of the board in order; that is, if a family is composed only of teenagers and adults, it would move only along Adolescent Lane and Adult Drive, omitting Primary Place. A family with preteens, teens, and adults would cover all three sides of the board.

If twenty-one stops are too time-consuming for your group, you may reduce the number of stops by assigning each family certain color squares. ("The Smiths will stop only on the blue, yellow, and orange squares.") But for the purposes of the game, *a family must visit the same color squares on each side*. A family may start on any square on any side of the board as long as it visits all of the assigned squares on one side before moving on to the next side.

Discussion

After participants have visited all assigned squares, have them all gather and sit together in families. Point out that on their answer sheets the three questions of each color form a horizontal grouping (blue: 1-8-15; red: 2-9-16; etc.).

In each of these groupings the same dilemma was posed in three different ways for three different age groups:

blue (1-8-15)—taking advantage of a unmonitored situation
red (2-9-16)—declining an invitation
yellow (3-10-17)—giving an opinion
green (4-11-18)—informing on someone else
orange (5-12-19)—using money designated for a specific purpose
black (6-13-20)—having someone "cover" for you
purple (7-14-21)—giving advice on honesty

If participants have responded differently to an issue for their own age category than they have for the other age categories, a double standard may be at work. ("It's okay for me to do that, but it's not okay for you!")

Have each family discuss the following questions among its own members and then report its conclusions to the total group.

1. Which decisions were the hardest for you to make? The easiest?
2. Which questions caused the greatest disagreement in your family? Which were the most readily agreed-upon ones?
3. What did you learn about your own double standards (what you believe is honest for you to do *vs.* what you believe is honest for others)?

Adapting the Game for Tabletop Use

Make the game board by gluing colored construction paper squares on a chalkboard or poster board base according to the positions shown in the diagram. Cut a slit in each construction paper square. Insert into this slit a small card on which the question has been typed.

If several families are to play, put several copies of the question into each square's slit.

Have each family choose a comfortable spot within the room as its discussion area. A family messenger will be sent to bring question cards, one at a time, from the table to the family.

Summary Activity: Answering the Question (5-10 minutes)

Purpose

To help families express their standards concerning honesty.

Instructions

Give each family a sheet of newsprint and a felt-tipped pen. Ask its members to answer this question: "When is honesty the best policy?" Share the results.

Closing (1-3 minutes)

Have participants join hands in a circle. Ask if anyone would like to comment on what he or she has learned during the session or what he or she felt to be positive about the session. The leader may add comments and then close with a prayer.

Thomas G. Bayes, Jr., is the associate minister of First Baptist Church in Madison, Wisconsin. He is a specialist in intergenerational education.
Terry J. Ging is the associate minister of the Grosse Pointe Congregational and American Baptist Church in Grosse Pointe, Michigan, with responsibility for youth programming.

DECISIONS

drugs: to use or not to use is not the only question

EXPLORING THE VARIETY OF USES OF DRUGS

Patricia C. Rondema

GOALS

To increase knowledge and awareness of different types of drugs. To open communication lines regarding drugs. To increase awareness of both good and bad uses of drugs. To increase awareness of individual responsibility in making decisions regarding drugs.

WHY?

People take drugs for many reasons. The same drug may have widely different effects when taken by different people in different situations, and there are many types of drugs. Our society is based on drug usage. No matter what your problem may be, there is a drug that can remedy your situation. If you can't sleep, have a cold, ate too much, are nervous, are upset, or just don't feel too happy, there is a pill or capsule or drink or concoction that will cure (or evade) all. The people in your group may or may not be experienced with many drugs. Most will have used some type of drug, aspirin, vaccine, etc. Some may have had some personal experience with one or more of the common drugs sold on the street. Regardless of their personal experiences, many will have had contact with people— at home, at school, or at church—who have had such experience. Every person in our society today has to deal with drugs and how he or she will personally respond to the choices offered to him or her. Both legal and illegal drugs are available to all, and each person must make choices as to if, when, how much, and for what reasons they will or will not use a particular drug.

NOTE TO LEADERS

When talking about drugs, it is necessary to keep in mind some guidelines for the discussion.

Scare tactics have not been effective in combating the use of even very addictive and dangerous drugs. Avoid such tactics.

Facts in the drug issue are sometimes confused. Depending upon whose research you examine, the effects of marijuana can vary widely. On many issues, highly respected people can drastically disagree. Many times youth can and will make a mature and caring response to highly volatile situations and issues regardless of what the facts or authorities seem to say. Since no one likes to be lectured, be careful to allow everyone the opportunity to share his or her ideas, feelings, and concerns. Everyone, including you, has that right.

Because there is a lot of slang language used regarding drugs, be sure everyone clarifies what he or she is talking about. It's likely that you may not be the only one who is not sure of the meaning of a word or phrase that has been used.

Be open to hearing both sides of an issue. In fact, try to have both sides of any question discussed. That helps everyone make a decision based on a fuller understanding of that issue.

Avoid generalizations. Lumping caffeine and heroin together may destroy whatever point a person is making.

The drug issue has been a hot one for many years. Part of the purpose of this session is to look at the drug scene without getting hot; to examine what drugs are, why they are used, what's good or bad about them; and to help all participants begin thinking about what their own responsibility is.

PREPARATION

Gather together large sheets of blank paper, marking pens or crayons, and writing paper. Write out role-play or buzz group topics.

PROCEDURE

Opening (10-15 minutes)

What kinds of drugs are there? What's good or bad about them? Have posted around the room large pieces of paper with phrases at the top. Participants are invited to complete or respond to them when they arrive. Some suggested phrases are listed below.
1. I think all drugs are. . . .
2. There are lots of drugs; for example. . . .
3. I'll never use . . . because. . . .
4. Drugs can be useful; for example. . . .
5. Drugs can be dangerous; for example. . . .
6. People use drugs because. . . .

When the group has gathered and everyone has had an opportunity to respond to the phrases, begin a group discussion of the phrases. Keep this brief; it is just a door opener. When discussing phrase 2, be sure the full range of drugs are mentioned. Include both medical (pain relieving, sleep inducing, consciousness altering, infection fighting, placebo) and social; legal (caffeine, nicotine, and alcohol if one is over the legal drinking age) and illegal (speed, heroin, marijuana, and alcohol if one is under the legal drinking age). When discussing phrases 4 and 5, try to round out the discussion. If no good or bad aspects of a particular drug have been voiced, try to fill that in yourself. Someone is probably thinking about it anyway. For example, morphine, a very powerful, addictive drug, was used during World War II to keep patients alive until treatment could be administered; cigarettes can help pacify a nervous person; marijuana is less fattening than alcohol. Have the group consider both sides of an issue. When discussing phrase 6, try to keep the discussion fairly specific. Don't lump widely different drugs together. Include both positive and negative reasons for the use of the drug.

Content (40-45 minutes)

Divide into small groups of four or five to develop a role play. Either assign, draw from a hat, or allow a maximum of five minutes to choose a topic (see list below). Allow about ten to fifteen minutes for preparation. Keep the groups informed of how the time is passing. Role plays can be presented continuously, followed by a discussion of them all, or they can be presented individually with a brief discussion following each. Watch the time so that all groups have a chance to present their work. Focus discussion on the needs of the people involved and how, as Christians and fellow human beings, we can respond.

Role-Play Situations

1. Group of teenage friends is at a home; parents are out; liquor is available; most want to drink.
2. Friend is using diet pills without doctor's or parents' knowledge. She or he looks sick, acts oddly. Group wants to help.
3. Mother uses a prescribed tranquilizer more often than the prescription recommends. She never talks to any of the family. Family wants real mother back.
4. Friend uses drugs (choose what kind or kinds). She or he has started cutting school and is having trouble relating to parents, siblings, friends. Group wants to help friend return to better times. (Friend may or may not be present in role play.)
5. Father comes home with a "don't-bother-me" attitude. He has a drink, watches television news, eats dinner, has a couple more drinks while reading the paper, and then falls asleep. Family needs to talk and relate to him.
6. Friend is having flashbacks from acid use. A frightening flashback happens at a home with just a few persons present. No adults know this friend has used acid.
7. Youth is arrested for possession of illegal drug. Parents pick him or her up at police station.
8. Student talks to parents about drinking alcohol. Parents are social drinkers. Student thinks his or her own drinking may be a problem but doesn't really want to (or can't) quit.
9. There is a group of youth, half of them users of marijuana and the other half opposed to its use. They talk with pastor or youth worker.
10. Family has one smoker. Others don't like the smell or mess.

Closure (10 minutes)

Give each person a piece of paper and a pencil. Have them complete each of the statements below silently. When all are ready, have them think about how drug use of any kind and specific kinds could affect what they have written. Allow time for anyone to share verbally if he or she so wishes. End with prayer asking for God's guidance in our decisions, especially regarding the choices that will be made concerning drugs and those who are having difficulty dealing with drugs.

Sentences to complete:
Happiness is. . . .
My greatest talent (strength, gift, skill) is. . . .
The three most important things in my life are. . . .

ADDITIONAL PROGRAM IDEAS

Choices

An activity which could be used after the opening might be a series of questions designed to bring out the difficulty of making choices, especially choices different from those of friends. Have everyone stand in the middle of the room. Have places in the room designated as choices A, B, and C. After the statement is read, each person then moves to the place that fits him or her best. Remember, each person has a right not to participate; but encourage all to make a choice. Following are some choices:

I'm more like (A) the mountains, (B) the ocean, (C) the plains.
I'm more like (A) a Mozart concerto, (B) a John Denver tune, (C) a Kiss album.
I'm more like (A) a rose, (B) a dandelion.
I'm more like (A) a group person, (B) a loner.
I'm more of (A) a leader, (B) a follower.

Allow a brief time to share why certain choices were made. When finished, briefly discuss how difficult it was to make some choices, especially if only one or two (or none) made that same choice. This activity should take about ten minutes, unless more choices are added.

Buzz Groups

If the group does not enjoy or do role plays, buzz groups can be substituted. The role-play situations can serve as topics, or some of the items below can be used.

Some feedback to the whole group should be given at the end. Use the same time format.
—Me, drugs, my future (work, family, children)
—Should marijuana be legalized?
—Is there a drug problem in our town? How does it affect us?
—What should I do if my friend is abusing drugs?
—Am I "my brother's keeper" regarding drugs since he or she chooses to take them himself or herself?
—Which is worse: tobacco, alcohol, marijuana?

Mural

Artistic or not-so-artistic members of the group might make a mural depicting the many types of drugs and their good and bad aspects. A large piece of butcher paper and drawing materials would be needed for this. It could be shared with other groups in the church.

Information

For some facts published by the government regarding drugs, you can call your local government information number and ask for referral to organizations that distribute this material.

Intergenerational

There are different types and degrees of drug usage; some may be beneficial to the user, his or her family, and society. Improper use may hurt health and relationships. Drug use involves moral issues and principles. The individual, the family, the church, and the community have responsibilities to prevent misuse and abuse of drugs. The program offered here could be used at most levels in the church. Adults as well as youth need to face the issues involved in the use of drugs in our society. We are all faced with these decisions daily.

Patricia C. Rondema is a junior high school math and English teacher. She has worked with junior high and senior high youth in her local congregation in Minneapolis, Minnesota, for most of the last ten years. She has served as a group leader and resource person in several national and international youth gatherings for the American Baptist Churches.

DECISIONS

stealing: a Christian perspective

LOOKING AT THE RESULTS OF STEALING   **Kenneth Potts**

GOAL

To look at the problem of stealing from a Christian perspective.

WHY?

At a junior high weekend retreat, the question of the "Christian" attitude toward stealing was raised. An informal poll revealed that *every* young person in attendance at the retreat had been faced at least once in the last six months with the decision of whether or not to participate in some sort of thievery—petty or major.

Though our statistical methods were not the most sophisticated, our results can probably be generalized to just about all junior high aged youth. Whether it's swiping candy bars at the grocery store or breaking into homes, stealing is a major problem for this age group.

Most junior-high-aged youth do not steal, but all are constantly faced with the temptation. Often that temptation is accompanied by almost overwhelming peer group pressure to "go along" and participate in some sort of group stealing. This is as true for Christian youth as it is for others. If Christian young people can deal with this issue in the context of a supportive Christian group, speaking about it openly and honestly, it is hoped that they can develop some guidelines that can be used in their day-to-day lives.

FACILITATING THE EXPERIENCE

Adult leaders do a great deal to influence the success of such a program. At this age level, youth are often shy and wary of revealing their true feelings, thoughts, and struggles. They know from experience that often adults will immediately condemn their views or interject unwanted advice.

During this program, it is important that the adult leader acts to reassure the participants that all their views will be accepted and valued. The leader must be careful not to contradict or belittle the opinions of the group members. It is also a good idea not to begin the experience by stating your own opinions; when the adult does so, it tends to produce an artificial concensus among the young people, who are usually wary of disagreeing with an adult. It is essential to the success of such an experience that the leader encourage all group members to contribute as many ideas as possible in an atmosphere of warmth and trust.

PREPARATION

A large area, inside or outside, needs to be available for the recreational activity.

Find out how long it takes an average youth to run the race described in Step 1.

An intimate study corner should be arranged for the exercises which follow the race in Step 1.

A number of large sheets of newsprint or a chalkboard should be situated in the study corner area. Following is a list of materials which should be assembled:

a stopwatch,

two boxes (at least ten inches square and an inch deep) labeled "A" and "B,"

one Ping Pong ball, large marble, or other easily carried item for *each* member of your group, plus an extra half dozen of the items

a suitable "prize" for the recreational activity (candy bars, pop, fruit, etc). Have a prize for each member of your group,

a copy of the case studies for each young person (if

this is not feasible, you might read the case studies to the group),

a number of large sheets of newsprint and a marker or a chalkboard and chalk,

a copy of the Bible.

PROCEDURE

Step 1: Recreation (20 minutes)

> ### WHY?
>
> Sometimes a point can be made by playing a game. The following race is designed to teach the group something about the results of stealing. By specifying certain instructions for each of the teams (in other words, by "rigging" the game), the group leaders will be providing an opportunity for the young people to experience directly the temptation to steal and the feeling of being robbed.
>
> The value in this approach is in the opportunity it provides for the group members to discuss their experiences immediately after they have occurred. Thoughts and emotions expressed will be the results of a "real" experience which will be fresh in their memories.

"A Rigged Run"

Lay out a course through your building, or outside the building, that can be safely run by the young people. It is important that the halfway point be hidden from sight of the starting line. At the halfway point, place two boxes.

Divide your group into two equal teams, "A" and "B." If you have an uneven number, one member of a team can run twice. Then place a Ping Pong ball (or other similar object) for each runner on team A in box A and likewise for team B.

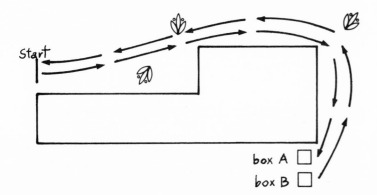

Explain to each team that the object of the game is for each team member to run to his or her team's box, grab a Ping Pong ball, and return to the start. So that the runners are not continually colliding with each other, team A will start first; the first runner for team B will start when team A's first runner is approximately halfway through the course. (This is why you need to have a stopwatch handy and why you need to know how long the average runner will take. If it is a two-minute course, start team B one minute after you start team A. This means, of course, that team A will have to finish *more* than one minute ahead of team B in order to win.) Each runner must bring back one, and only one, Ping Pong ball to prove that he or she ran the entire course. The first team to have all runners complete the course, each runner bringing back a Ping Pong ball, wins and is awarded a prize.

Now we come to the "rigging" of our race. So that they can familiarize themselves with the course, send all members of team B to survey the course. Suggest that they might discuss various strategies for running. While team B is occupied, instruct team A as follows:

"There is only one Ping Pong ball in team B's box for each runner. If a member of your team (team A) were to steal one of the Ping Pong balls from box B instead of taking his or her ball from box A, team B would not be able to finish the race. It could not win fairly, and your team (team A) would not have to worry about running fast. It is entirely up to you (the members of team A) whether or not you steal a ball from team B."

Make no other comment about these instructions; reread them to team A if necessary. After you have completed instructing team A, send its members to survey the course.

When both teams have returned, secretly send a confederate to the boxes and have him or her transfer one of team B's Ping Pong balls to box A, also adding six or more extra balls to box A.

As the race is run, some interesting dynamics are possible:

team A will be faced with a group decision as to whether or not to steal;

each runner for team A will arrive at the halfway point alone, with the opportunity to guarantee the outcome of the race;

at least the last runner for team B, if not the last few runners, will find no Ping Pong balls in box B, but extra balls in box A.

As the race nears an end, it will become evident if it has been run fairly. As soon as it is obvious that something is wrong, stop the race, give *everyone* a prize, and move to the study corner.

Debriefing "A Rigged Run"

First, explain that the race was rigged and how it was done. Stress the fact that members of team A were given permission to steal (this is necessary to prevent any hard feelings between the teams). Then, as a group work through the following questions:

How did team A decide whether or not to steal from team B (was it an individual or a group decision)?

Did everyone agree, or were there differences of opinion?

Was stealing okay because an older person suggested it?

What feelings did the members of team A have when they reached the boxes?

When did team B discover that it did not have enough Ping Pong balls?

Who discovered this?

How did this person feel?

What did this person decide to do?

What were the overall results of stealing (the team members' or the confederate's) on the game?

Don't try to bring the group to a conclusion about the ethics of stealing just yet; right now you are gathering information and exploring feelings. After the group members have worked through these questions, ask them to remember their experiences and reactions so that they can talk about them later.

Step 2: Two Short Case Studies (10 minutes)

Following are two case studies. Ask each person to read through Case Study I (or read the case study to the group if you have only one copy). Next, as a group, list as many possible options as you can think of for Bill (you should write these down on newsprint or chalkboard). *Don't* worry about whether an option is "right" or "wrong." The goal is to list as many options as possible.

When you have completed the listing of options for Case Study I, move on to Case Study II and repeat the process. Save both of these lists.

WHY?

This particular exercise is designed to take the young person through a step-by-step process of decision making, to show youth that there is a logical way to deal with this situation, and to introduce the youth to a specifically Christian way of analyzing a complex situation and choosing the best course of action from among the many alternatives.

Case Study I

Bill, Ann, and Sam were good friends. They were spending the weekend, along with other friends, at a retreat sponsored by the church. Sam brought along his tape player and quite a few tapes, which he continually left out for anyone to see and use.

Bill and Sam had gone for a walk. As they were returning to the lodge, Sam stopped for a moment to talk to one of the sponsors. Bill went ahead, entering the lodge. The building was empty except for Ann. As Bill walked into the room, he saw her quickly stuffing some of Sam's tapes into her suitcase.

At the sound of the screen door slamming behind Bill, Ann looked up, startled. She looked at him for what seemed like ages, though it was only a few seconds. Both of them knew full well that she had been stealing Sam's tapes.

Before Bill or Ann could say anything to each other, they heard Sam calling Bill's name. He was approaching the lodge. There was no way that Bill and Ann would have time to talk before Sam entered; nor was there time for Ann to put the tapes back, though she did have time to shut the suitcase with the tapes in it and hide it under the bed if Bill would let her.

Case Study II

Bill stopped by the sports shop on his way to work to pick up some Ping Pong balls to take to the youth group meeting that night. He was in a hurry, as he didn't want to be late for work; so he did not wait for a clerk but went to the correct aisle himself. As he rounded the corner of the shelving, he saw Jim and Frank, good friends of his, attempting to stuff five or six handballs quickly into their pockets. They were startled by Bill's sudden appearance but still managed quickly to pocket the handballs. Then Jim grabbed another handful and shoved them at Bill. "Here, hide these, quick!"

A split second later, a clerk, who had not seen any of what had happened, called from the next aisle, "Hey, need any help?"

Step 3: Bringing in a Christian Perspective (20 minutes)

There are two basic objectives in this step: first, to establish that a Christian ethic generally prohibits stealing, and second, to help the junior high youth understand why this is so.

WHY?

"But isn't it enough simply to say, 'You shouldn't steal'?" you may be asking.

Not really. For this age group it is important to develop a sense of understanding about why a particular action is right or wrong. Junior high youth are not content simply to be told what is right or wrong; they want—and need—to understand what is behind a decision. The process here is designed to show the young person both what is generally considered to be the Christian ethical position *and* what reasoning lies behind that position.

Read to the group the following passages (if possible, use a fairly modern translation, such as the *Good News Bible* or *The New English Bible*):

Deuteronomy 5:1, 19
Leviticus 19:13-14
Proverbs 21:6-7
Ephesians 4:28
Romans 13:9

Point out to the group that these passages have always been interpreted by Christians to mean that stealing is not right. This, then, is generally the Christian position.

Next, read to the group the following New Testament passages:

Matthew 22:34-40
John 13:34-35
1 John 4:19-21
Colossians 3:12-14

Jesus talks about a certain value—love—which Christians have at the center of their lives. The passages in the New Testament letters show that the first Christians took Jesus very seriously about this.

Jesus' commandment to love can help us as we look at stealing. We're searching for the "why" to the Christian position that stealing is wrong. If we can show that stealing is not loving, then we can conclude

that there is a very good reason for Christians to consider it wrong.

Take the time to discuss as a group how stealing can be unloving. Ask the group to point out how stealing hurts other people. (You might ask the group to recall its experience with "A Rigged Run.")

Finally, go back to the two lists of options developed for Case Study I and Case Study II. Ask the group to choose those options which are consistent with a Christian ethic, i.e., are most loving. As the group struggles with these decisions, the question should be raised as to what options Bill could choose that would be most loving for the individuals caught stealing. This is also an important question and should be thoroughly discussed from the context of a Christian ethic (it is undoubtedly a question which will arise in real life for these youth).

Step 4: The Peer Group (5 minutes)

We have one more issue to touch on as we talk about the problem of stealing—peer group pressure. This is a diffucult subject, especially since the junior-high-aged youth is very susceptible to such pressure.

Begin this discussion by asking the group to define what peer group pressure is; point out how overwhelming it can be. Then ask the group to list as many ways as they can think of to stand up for a Christian ethic when they are with a group of youth who are involved in stealing. It can be helpful if the leader takes the time to write these ideas on a sheet of newsprint or chalkboard as they are suggested.

Step 5: Applying What We've Learned (5 minutes)

Our program has centered around a few particular situations in which a junior-high-aged youth might be involved. Our next step is to try to generalize our learning to a variety of possible situations.

Ask the group to suggest as many situations as they can think of in which they might be faced with the decision whether or not to steal. List these on the newsprint or chalkboard.

Suggest to the group that they might try to use what they have learned in their experience with this program as they are faced with these decisions.

Step 6: A Closing Thought (5 minutes)

Remind the group that as Christians, we believe that we can call on God to assist us in living the Christian life-style. Talking to God is not just something we do at meals or before we go to sleep; we should do so in the midst of the difficult situations in which we are involved. This includes the times when we are faced with the temptation to steal. End this program with a short sentence prayer or silent prayer asking for God's wisdom, courage, and strength as we struggle with the problem of stealing.

ADDITIONAL PROGRAM IDEAS

For Step 2: As a group, write your own case study illustrating the problem of stealing.

For Step 3: To help establish the damage that stealing does, assign interview teams of two or more youth to talk to the following people:

  a school principal
  a downtown merchant
  a local policeman
  a probation officer
  a grocery store manager

Draw up a list of questions for each interview team to use, centering on how stealing affects the organization or business in which the individual is involved. Have your teams bring the results of their interviews to be discussed at your next meeting.

For Step 4: Develop a role play which centers on a young person trying to resist peer group pressure to steal.

RESOURCES

There are a number of publications dealing with these particular techniques: *Beginning Values Clarification: A Guide for the Use of Values Clarification in the Classroom* by Sidney B. Simon and Jay Clark (La Mesa, Calif.: Pennant Press, 1975), *Value Clarification as Learning Process: A Sourcebook for Educators* by Brian P. Hall (New York: Paulist Press, 1974), *Integrating Values* by Louis M. Savary (Dayton, Ohio: Pflaum/Standard, 1974), and *Values and Faith: Value Clarifying Exercises for Family and Church Groups* by Roland and Doris Larson (Minneapolis: Winston Press, Inc., 1976) are all excellent books introducing the values-clarification approach; *Value Exploration Through Role Playing* by Robert C. Hawley (New York: Hart Publishing Co., Inc., 1974) is a basic exploration of the use of role playing in groups.

As a rule of thumb, the more research that is done into how and why we use a particular technique, the more effectively we will be able to use it.

Kenneth Potts is a minister at the First Baptist Church of La Grange, Illinois, with responsibilities in Christian education and youth programming.

DECISIONS

making tough decisions

DISCOVERING TOOLS FOR MAKING DECISIONS   Kenneth Potts

GOAL

To discover and use some tools for making wise decisions in a Christian context.

WHY?

As they grow older, youth are increasingly faced with difficult decisions. Many of these situations were thought in the past to be concerns only of high school and older youth: drinking, smoking, dating and sexual experimentation, drug use, stealing, cheating in school. With the increasing complexity in our society, however, many of these situations which require difficult decisions are now part of the world of the junior high youth. At the same time, this age group often lacks the experience and maturity to make rational decisions.

Also, because of the complexity of our society, absolute answers—yes or no—are rarely accepted. What is needed is to provide young people with the tools to evaluate a situation, their feelings about it, and the possible consequences of certain actions. These tools enable young people to make their own decisions—which they will do anyway—but, it is hoped, in an intelligent and Christian context.

FACILITATING THE EXPERIENCE

Adult leaders can do a great deal to influence the success of this experience. Junior high youth are quite often shy and many times wary of revealing their own inner struggles and thoughts before an adult. They know from experience that often adults will imme-

diately condemn their views or interject unwanted advice.

An adult leader will be most helpful in an experience such as this when he or she acts to reassure the junior high youth that *all* their views will be accepted and valued. This means that the leader must be careful not to contradict or belittle the opinions of the young person. Nor should the leader begin the exercise by stating his or her own opinion; this tends to produce an artificial consensus among the young people, who are wary of disagreeing with an adult. Rather, the leader should encourage all group members to contribute as many ideas as possible in an atmosphere of warmth and trust. This is essential to the success of such an experience.

PREPARATION

In preparing for this session, it might be helpful if the group leader became familiar with the techniques involved. Four distinct methods of working toward our goal are used: a recreational activity which centers on decision making; a values-clarification exercise centering on the steps in decision making; a role play involving the results of the exercise; and a brainstorming session to help the young people see the applications of what they have experienced in their day-to-day living.

The room should be arranged as described below, or plans could be made to move from room to room to achieve the desired setting. Another possibility is to make plans to change the room arrangement quickly and efficiently between segments of the program.

—A large area needs to be cleared for the recreational activity.

—The leader should become familiar with the case study by reading it through a number of times, working to make the reading of it as lively and dramatic as possible.

—An intimate study corner could be arranged for the case study reading and exercise.

—An area which simulates a classroom seating arrangement would add to the realism of the role play.

—A large sheet of newsprint or a chalkboard should be situated in the study corner area.

Following is a list of materials which should be assembled prior to the session:

a large, soft playground ball or beach ball,

a copy of the case study,

a copy of the worksheet for each group member (see the sample sheet included),

a writing instrument for each group member,

a copy of the Bible for each group member,

a large sheet of newsprint and markers or a chalkboard and chalk.

PROCEDURE

"Confusion Hockey" (10 minutes)

Clear a large area. The two walls at each end of this area will serve as goals (you might mark off an area on each wall about twelve feet long and four feet high to serve as limits to the scoring areas, or you can use the whole wall as a scoring area). The members of the group should gather in the center of the room. There are *no* organized teams. Individuals can choose to try to score in either of the two goals, or both; they can defend one of the goals, or both; they can work alone, in pairs, in groups, change sides, etc. There are no rules except those prohibiting roughness, tripping, pushing, and so on. No score will be kept by a scorekeeper. Start the game by dropping the ball in the center of the room. It can only be kicked, not picked up or handled. Play lasts for five minutes. Stress to the players that they are *not* to talk to one another during the game. (This makes it more difficult to organize teams of any kind.)

WHY?

Why play a game which seems to have little organization and few guidelines? Mainly because it parallels many of the situations in real life in which young people find themselves involved. In "Confusion Hockey" the junior high youth are quickly forced to make a series of decisions with

---

a minimum of guidance and information. "Do I try to score?" "Do I defend a goal?" "Why?" "Should I help another player?" "Can I trust another player to help me?" After five minutes of participating in such a game, players will have a wealth of feelings and thoughts to share with one another about making decisions.

Debriefing "Confusion Hockey"

This game will have provided the youth with a number of experiences in decision making. Sharing these experiences will help to introduce the rest of the session. Call the young people together in the study corner and talk about the following questions:

What was the goal of the game?

How did you decide that goal was the goal?

Did you team up with someone or play alone?

How did you decide with whom to team up?

Did you try to score or try to defend a goal?

How did you decide which one to do and when to do it?

Sometimes a game is designed to show you something. What might this game be trying to show you?

A Case Study and Values-Clarification Exercise (25 minutes)

Read the following case study to the youth. Let yourself be dramatic; try to involve your listeners in the emotions of the story.

Carrie was really upset. She had studied hard for the test and wanted to do a good job. Now as the test lay in front of her, half finished, she found that she just couldn't concentrate.

Mrs. Johnson, her teacher, had left the room two minutes ago when she had been called to the office. Her parting words had been to "keep your eyes on your own paper, please." Yet the second she was out the door, the two boys in front of Carrie had started comparing answers. Soon, most of the rest of the class had joined in. Carrie felt that she was the only student who wasn't taking part in the cheating.

Suddenly, the boy in front of Carrie turned around and said, "Hey, Carrie, you're a brain! What did you put down for number twelve?"

That was the hardest question on the test. Carrie had studied a lot to be ready for just that question. Now the whole class turned expectantly to her. A girl two seats over chimed in, "Yeah, nobody knows that one. What's the answer, Carrie?"

There was total silence in the room. The other students waited for her reply. What would she do?

After you have read the preceding case study, check out the facts with your group. Does everyone understand the situation? Once any questions have been cleared up, go on to the worksheet.

Each young person should have a full-page copy of the worksheet and a pen or pencil. As a group, have the young people list as many possible options for Carrie (things she could do in the situation) as they can think of. *Don't* worry about "right" or "wrong." The object of this step is to compile as large a list of options as possible.

WHY?

A worksheet such as this is designed to take youth through a step-by-step process of decision making. It shows young people that there is a logical way to deal with the tough decisions which they face. This exercise will also introduce the youth to a specifically Christian way of analyzing a complex situation and choosing the best course of action from among many alternatives.

After the group members have listed as many options for Carrie as they can think of, go back through the worksheet and decide how each of these options would affect the major characters in the case study. For example, let's say that one of the options listed by the group is to "ignore the rest of the class." Ask your young people to think about how choosing this option would affect Carrie. It might make her feel left out, anxious about whether or not the class would continue to like her, but glad she didn't cheat. List these under the column entitled "Effect on Carrie." Next, talk about the effect choosing this option would have on the other members of the class. For instance, it might make them feel angry and perhaps a little guilty about their actions. It might cause them to admire Carrie for her stand. List these effects in the appropriate column on the worksheet. This particular option would probably not affect Mrs. Johnson; so leave that part blank. Then move to the next option and repeat the process. Do this with all the options you have listed. See the sample worksheet for an example of what this might look like.

So far, your group has seen that there are a number of options open to a person in a given situation and that selecting any one of these possible options will affect in some way the people involved. The next step is actually to choose one of these options.

WORKSHEET

Option	Effect on Carrie	Effect on Class	Effect on Mrs. Johnson
1. Ignore the rest of the class.	Make her feel left out; alone; anxious; glad she didn't cheat.	Make them angry; make them feel guilty; admire Carrie.	Probably none.

Give to each young person a copy of the New Testament (a fairly modern translation, such as the *Good News Bible* or *The New English Bible,* would be best). Direct the youth to the following passages:

> Matthew 22:34-40
> John 13:34-35
> 1 John 4:19-21
> Colossians 3:12-14

In the Gospels of Matthew and John, Jesus seems to be talking about a certain value which we should have at the center of our lives. That value is love. This was the new and all-important commandment for Jesus' followers. From the passages from the New Testament letters, one sees that members of the early church took Jesus very seriously on this point, seeking to order their entire lives around this central commandment.

Jesus' commandment can help us in our decision making. If we are to love others, then we can (and should) decide to do whatever is *most loving* for all the people involved in a situation. Now we have a Christian value which we can apply in those situations in which we are forced to make difficult decisions. Take a few minutes and point out to your group how this value—loving others—is brought out in each of the passages listed above. Suggest to them that they might use such a value as a basis for making difficult decisions such as the one which Carrie faces. What if Carrie were to decide to do whatever is most loving for all the people involved?

Go back to the worksheet. Ask each young person to circle the option which he or she thinks is most loving. You might phrase your directions like this: "Of all the things we've listed that Carrie might do, which do you think would be the most loving thing to do for *all* the people involved?"

After each young person has chosen the option which he or she believes is most loving in the situation; discuss their choices. Make sure to do so in a non-threatening manner. Do not impose your opinion on the group; wait until all members of the group have had

a chance to share their ideas before *offering* your understanding. After everyone has shared his or her opinion, have the group members choose one option that they feel is one of the most loving. You will use this option as a basis for a short role play.

A Short Role Play (10 minutes)

Now is a good time for a change of pace activity that will involve some action. Assemble the group in the area simulating a classroom. Ask for volunteers to play the parts of Carrie and the other major characters in the case study. Other young people can play the part of the other class members. Have the group recreate the case study up until the point where Carrie is faced with her decision; then have the group act out the option which it has selected. As soon as the role play has seemed to reach a natural stopping point, stop the group and debrief. You might use the following questions as a way of doing this:

> How do each of you (the characters) feel (what emotions are you experiencing)?
> What feelings do you (the characters) have about one another?
> Did the option that you acted out result in the effects that you thought it would?
> Is it an option that you would be willing to try if you were in a similar situation in real life?

Applying What We've Learned (5 minutes or more)

Gather again in the study corner. On the large sheet of newsprint, have the group members list as many possible situations as they can think of in which they might use this approach to making decisions. These situations might involve drinking, smoking, dating, sexual experimentation, drug use, personal honesty, etc. Let the young people take as much time as they need to explore the potential uses of this approach. End by challenging your junior high youth to try this Christian approach to decision making at least once in the coming week.

ADDITIONAL PROGRAM IDEAS

Before the Session

The week before you use "Making Tough Decisions" ask your young people to find as many articles as they can in magazines and newspapers which concern people who have to make really difficult decisions. Have them cut these articles out and bring them to the meeting. Talk about why these decisions are difficult.

Another Game for Outdoors

Another recreational activity involves using a large "earth ball" or "cage ball" (probably available in one of your area schools). Put the ball in a large grassy area and pick two goals. The object of the game is to push the ball over either of the goal lines. As with "Confusion Hockey" no teams are selected. Game players decide where and when to push the ball and whether to defend either of the goals. Debrief in the same manner as "Confusion Hockey."

A Different Case Study

A number of other case study situations can develop out of the imaginations of your youth. Ask them to design their own stories about young people in difficult situations. They might want to go through a worksheet on one of these situations.

Another source of case studies is the Old and New Testaments. Ask your youth to pick out stories from the Bible that involve characters in situations in which they are faced with tough decisions.

Your more artistic youth might enjoy illustrating a case study (the one given about Carrie or one of their own) in comic-book style. Not so artistic young people could help with the dialogue, layout, etc.

Other Role Plays

A number of role plays can be developed around the theme of decision making. For example: a lifeboat has only enough room for four people; any more will swamp the boat. Nine people are in the water. You have to decide who will survive by getting in the lifeboat. There are countless similar situations which lend themselves to a discussion on tough decisions and this approach.

Personal Decision Making

Prior to listing the possible tough decisions that they face, young people might be asked to list individually all the tough decisions that they have already made in the past week. These could be discussed.

An Extra Activity

As a final group activity, board games such as "Monopoly" or "Aggravation" which involve decision making might be adapted to suit our purposes. Instruct the players to use the Christian value of loving the other players as they make decisions throughout the game. This might mean not charging rent to a poorer player when he or she lands on your property or perhaps not sending a person back to start if he or she is having a rough time; the possibilities are endless.

To Do at Home

Ask group members to ask their parents how they make tough decisions. Have the young people report back at the next meeting.

Ask group members to pay special attention to the TV programs they watch in the coming week. Have them list three shows which involve the shows' characters in making tough decisions. Discuss these at the next meeting.

RESOURCES

See the resources mentioned at the end of the previous program.

As a rule of thumb, the more research that is done into how and why we use a particular technique, the more effectively we will be able to use it.

Kenneth Potts is a minister at the First Baptist Church of La Grange, Illinois, with responsibilities in Christian education and youth programming.

LIFE-STYLE
LIFE-STYLE
LIFE-STYLE

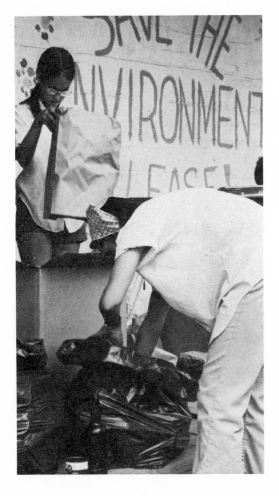

LIFE-STYLE

LIFE-STYLE

salad bowl

RECALLING CULTURAL HERITAGE Donald T-M Ng

GOALS

To help junior high youth recall their cultural heritages in light of the gospel and to appreciate that identity in our pluralistic society.

WHY?

With the exception of the native American Indians, each of us has cultural heritages from other lands. These heritages are rich with traditions which enable a person to answer a basic question: "Where do I come from?" We can understand ourselves better as we attempt to recall our past with pride.

If cultural traditions from another country are missing, perhaps our life has been affected by the portion of this country our family calls home. Have we descended from Western pioneers, from New England Yankees, or from Southerners? Has a specific descent affected what we have become?

The uniqueness of each individual needs to be expressed to reveal the multiplicity and interdependence of today's world. In 1 Corinthians 12:12-27 we are told to appreciate the many gifts and differences of our fellow Christians: "For just as the body is one and has many members . . . so it is with Christ" (verse 12).

PREPARATION

Materials: copies of the "family tree," found at the end of this program, for each person*
newsprint or chalkboard with the questions in Step 2 printed on it.
felt markers or chalk
all the things that make a good salad (lettuce, tomatoes, etc.)

*Note: You may want to pass out copies of the "family tree" a week early so your youth can ask their parents or other relatives for some of the information. This would be helpful for those who do not know much of their family history and would also encourage an intergenerational experience.

PROCEDURE

Step 1: Where Do I Come From? (15 minutes)

Gather your group together to introduce the program by asking if any have seen or read Alex Haley's *Roots*. Share briefly with the group your own feelings on the question "Where do I come from?"

Give each person a "family tree" chart to fill out. Encourage him or her to fill in names and facts in the appropriate boxes and spaces as best as he or she can. (Skip this part if the youth have filled out the charts at home.)

Step 2: Free at Last (30 minutes)

WHY?

God wants us to be ourselves, living up to our potentials and desires. However, many of us have been made to be ashamed of our past histories in place of being more Americanized. By sharing our family trees, we are freed from our inhibitions and fears, and we are affirming our past.

Divide the total group into small groups of three to share the charts. Have members of the same family take different groups. Give each person ten minutes to tell about his or her chart. Have the following questions printed on newsprint or chalkboard to help stimulate discussion:

1. Can you remember or do you know of family members coming to America?
2. Do you still have relatives living in another country?
3. What does your surname mean?
4. Does your family practice any cultural traditions that are considered to be brought over from another country? How do you feel about them?
5. If your family has lived in this country for several generations, are you aware of regional traditions or influences which have affected your life-style and values?
6. What types of food does your family generally eat? Do they reflect a certain cultural background?
7. Were there areas of your life that you have not shared with anyone before now? Why haven't you?

Step 3: Members of One Body (10 minutes)

Remaining in the small groups, look up 1 Corinthians 12:12-27 for a Bible study. Guide the study with the following questions:

1. Since it is possible to speak of arms, eyes, ears, etc., as parts of a body, how do you feel about being different from one another but remaining as a part of the whole?
2. What does it mean that "by one Spirit we were all baptized into one body"?

Step 4: Closing (5 minutes)

Have the group come back together so that you can share the following thoughts: As God has arranged the different parts of the body to work together as an integrated whole, God sees each of us as uniquely different but joined together by one Spirit: Jesus Christ. The image of the "melting pot" has, therefore, given way to that of the "salad bowl." It takes all the different ingredients to make up a salad; the ingredients remain, nonetheless, lettuce, tomatoes, cucumbers, etc. What binds them together is the salad dressing. Similarly, faith in Christ binds us together.

Have each person bring an ingredient for a salad. Make a salad out of these ingredients and bless it as representative of who we are. Have the salad as the refreshment for the evening.

SUPPLEMENTAL RESOURCES (all prices subject to change)

For white Americans

Fackre, Gabriel J., *Liberation in Middle America.* New York: United Church Press, 1971. Hardback, $4.95.

Novak, Michael, *The Rise of the Unmeltable Ethnics.* New York: Macmillan, Inc., 1972. Hardback, $7.95.

For Asian Americans

Nagano, Paul, comp., *My Spiritual Pilgrimages.* Seattle, Wash.: Asian American Baptist Caucus, 1976. Available through the caucus, 901 E. Spruce St., Seattle, WA 98122. Paperback, $2.00.

Tachiki, Amy, ed., *Roots: An Asian American Reader.* Berkeley: The Regents of the University of California, 1971. Paperback, $5.50.

For black Americans

Haley, Alex, *Roots.* New York: Doubleday & Co., Inc., 1976. Paperback, $2.75.

Mitchell, Henry H., *Black Belief.* New York: Harper & Row, Publishers, 1975. Hardback, $7.95.

For native Americans

Gridley, Marion E., *Contemporary American Indian Leaders.* New York: Dodd, Mead & Company, 1972. Hardback, $4.95.

Steiner, Stan, *The New Indians*. New York: Dell Publishing Co., Inc., 1969. Paperback, $2.65.

For Hispanic Americans

Steiner, Stan, *La Raza: The Mexican Americans*. New York: Harper & Row, Publishers, 1969. Paperback, $1.95.

Wakefield, Dan, *Island in the City: The World of Spanish Harlem*. New York: Arno Press, Inc., 1960. Paperback, $1.75.

Donald T-M Ng has been minister of Christian education at the First Chinese Baptist Church, San Francisco, California, with staff responsibility for youth ministries. He is now program associate in the Department of Ministry with Youth, Board of Educational Ministries, American Baptist Churches in the U.S.A.

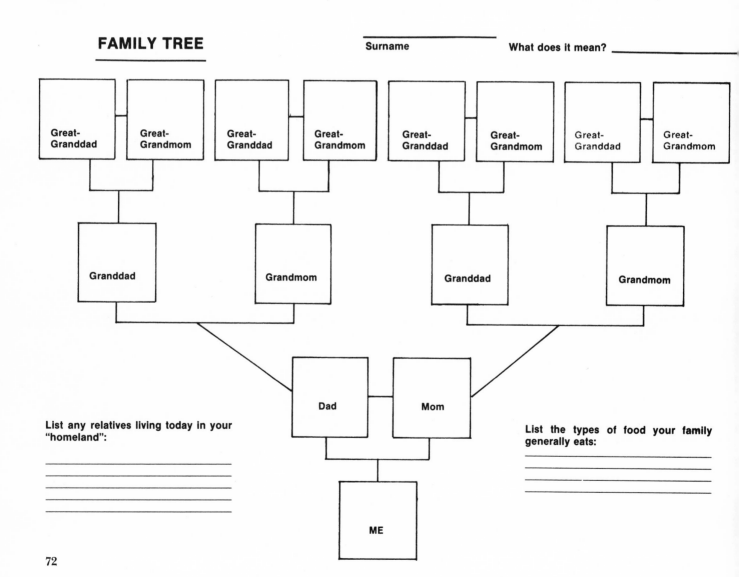

LIFE-STYLE

in search of freedom

SHARING THE BLACK EXPERIENCE   **Classie Murray**

America is a composite of people and their contributions. Cultural awareness will help junior highs to appreciate the differences in others and also see how those differences as well as similarities contribute to the wholeness of America. Just as the fixings in the salad are unique, each adding color and variety to the dish, so do the cultural heritages of ethnic groups add color and variety to our society.

The activities in this program are based on the black experience. However, they may be adapted for any ethnic group. A cultural awareness week (a series)—including studies about American Indians, Asian Americans, and Spanish Americans—could do much to bridge the cultural gap.

HERITAGE—WHAT IS IT?

Making an Acrostic

> ### WHY?
>
> The use of a word game will help to stimulate thinking about the meaning of cultural heritage and all that it implies.

Materials

newsprint, felt-tipped markers (assorted colors), crayons, tape

Procedure

1. Divide the group if more than ten are present.
2. Each group is to define "heritage" by making an acrostic and arriving at a definition of heritage from the words. (Note sample.)

H omes
E veryone
R eligion
I deas
T raditions
A rt, ancestors
G ames
E yes

3. Allow ten minutes for making the acrostic and arriving at a definition.
4. One person from each small group can share the group's findings with the total group. Note the similarities and differences in acrostics.
5. Each group's work might be put on display.

Have a Black-Afro Treasure Hunt

> ### WHY?
>
> Blacks are a distinctive part of the people salad. Their cultural roots and racial pride go back to their rich African heritage. From this source black influence can be traced to America's beginning.

Materials

large sheets of construction paper, poster board, stapler, masking tape, markers, items related to black culture

Procedure

1. Have the group construct a large container of symbolic nature in which items related to black culture can be placed.

2. Individuals are to bring these items that are representative of black culture. The group could make a list of categories from which each person would choose the item he or she will bring. Categories could include literature, art, dance, musical instruments, writers, etc.

3. Before placing it in the container, each person can share the sample or replica he or she has brought that has historical or family significance. Food considered "soul food" might be brought and served to the group as a treat.

Closure—Worship

Have the group sit in a circle and spend a few moments sharing new discoveries. They may also want to make plans for another cultural awareness program.

Then have one person who has been asked ahead of time read 1 John 4:21 from *The Living Bible*. Then play the sermon "I Have a Dream" by Dr. Martin Luther King, Jr. (The record "In Search of Freedom" contains this sermon and may be obtained from the public library.)

ADDITIONAL PROGRAM IDEAS

Black Music

WHY?

Music is a universal language, and it's an expression of the era of the people who write it.

Materials

song sheets, song leader, record player, records (sacred, classical, spirituals, jazz, etc.), puppets, stage (table on its side, back of a sofa, puppet stage)

Puppet Show

Puppets could do a medley of songs (ad lib with records) that are part of the black heritage. A simple skit done by the puppets could give a brief history of spirituals, of a song writer, or of a message which a song conveys. An old-fashioned singspiration would be a good climax to this program. A guitarist or versatile pianist would insure the success of the program. Use local black musicians or a song leader.

Note: Puppetry is a new but fast-growing ministry. Youths could make puppets or purchase them in their area. I recommend Puppets Productions, Box 82200, San Diego, CA 92138. Puppets, scripts, cassette tapes, and a stage can be purchased, though they are very expensive.

Youth Musical

Local youths could plan and present a musical presentation which includes songs of all cultures.

Love Feast

To culminate your cultural awareness series, plan a love feast and serve a variety of ethnic foods. Junior highs might use puppets to share some of their cultural discoveries, and artwork could be displayed.

RESOURCES (all prices subject to change)

Bryan, Ashley, *Walk Together Children*. New York: Atheneum Publishers, 1974. $7.95.
A collection of black American spirituals that includes both words and music.

Contemporary Art by Afro-Americans. New York: Friendship Press, n.d., $1.75.

D'Amato, Janet and Alex, *African Crafts for You to Make*. New York: Julian Messner, 1969. $6.29.
The customs of tribes are combined with directions for making replicas of African objects.

Hughes, Langston, *Don't You Turn Back*. Edited by Lee B. Hopkins. New York: Alfred A. Knopf, Inc., 1969. $5.69.
A sensitive selection of poems expressing the black experience in America with striking illustrations.

Johnson, J. W. and J. R., eds., *Books of American Negro Spirituals*. New York: Da Capo Press, Inc., 1977. $7.95.

Portraits of Twentieth-Century Afro-Americans. New York: Friendship Press, n.d., $1.75.
Large (10″ x 14″) photographs of twenty-four outstanding blacks, such as Martin Luther King, Marian Anderson, Thurgood Marshall, Constance Cook, Ralph Bunche, etc.

Stokes, Olivia P., *The Beauty of Being Black: Folktales, Poems and Art from Africa*. Edited by Louise Crane. New York: Friendship Press, 1970. $2.50.

_____, *Why the Spider Lives in Corners: African Facts and Fun*. Edited by Louise Crane. New York: Friendship Press, 1971. $2.25.
Stories, folktales, songs, and games from Africa.

Classie Murray is a member and former youth sponsor of the First Baptist Church, Springfield, Illinois.

LIFE-STYLE

roots and traditions

EXPLORING FAMILY BACKGROUNDS INTERGENERATIONALLY   Kenneth C. Whitt

GOALS

To learn about the importance of a family's roots and traditions and to discuss our various backgrounds, knowing that such sharing can bring both individual families and larger groups closer together.

WHY?

The book and television movie *Roots* by Alex Haley have brought sharply to mind the importance of knowing where we have come from in order to know who we are and where we are going. This is certainly not a new insight to people who know the Old Testament, which continually recalls the covenant relationship of God and the people of the nation of Israel, the descendants of Abraham, Issac, and Jacob (e.g., Deuteronomy 29).

But in our highly mobile society, with its emphasis on newness and change, families easily lose touch with their past, and even the significant traditions of the previous generation are lost. Our family and personal lives could be enriched by knowledge of our past.

PREPARATION

You will need a large world map and a large United States map. (They may be found in old issues of *National Geographic.*) Have three different colors of yarn, as well as paper, pencils, tape, and thumbtacks if you are going to put the maps on a bulletin board. Before the program, read Deuteronomy 29 and/or other related passages in order to become more aware of how important the history of past generations was to the people of Israel. Reading a commentary might be helpful. Also, be prepared to present your own responses to the exercises below (see Step 2), possibly by having the experience with your family in advance.

PROCEDURE

Introduction

You may want to introduce this program by sharing some ideas from the "Why?" box above and from your own reading as suggested under "Preparation." You might read parts of Deuteronomy 29 or talk about the important role ancestors played in the religious faith of the people of Israel. (Even today their history is recalled by Jewish families celebrating religious festivals like the Passover.)

WHY?

The idea that roots and traditions matter may seem strange to persons in our mobile society, but to recall the importance they played in earlier times may be helpful to the group members looking at their individual roots.

Step 1

Ask each family present to meet together and share as much information as it can about its family roots. Find out specifically:
  a. Birthplace of parents,
  b. Birthplace of grandparents,
  c. Country or countries of origin of the family.
Have each family discuss together all the information it has about its family's roots and write down its answers.

WHY?

The family discussion may bring out information its members had never talked about before, encouraging family dialogue and possibly further research.

Step 2

Bring the group back together; the program leader should share the information of his or her family. Indicate with the yarn (stretching it from one point to the other on the maps) the roots of your family. For example,

Red yarn—from the birthplace of grandparents to the ancestral home (e.g., Germany, Ghana, Japan),

Blue yarn—from the birthplace of parents to birthplace of grandparents,

White yarn—from the birthplace of parents to the present home.

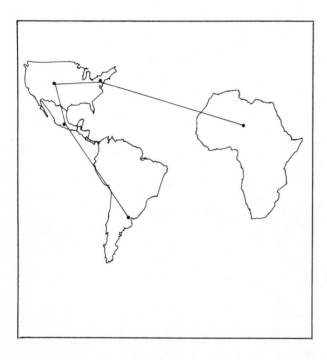

WHY?

Sharing by the leader can make the instructions to the families clearer and set a level for sharing by the participants. Using the maps and the yarn will give the group members a visual aid to see clearly the richness of their various backgrounds and will make the sharing of their roots more meaningful.

Step 3

Have each of the families take the information it discussed and place it on the map, as in Step 2.

Step 4

Have one person from each family summarize briefly for the rest of the group the most important information from his or her family.

WHY?

Sharing this important information about their families can help them appreciate the uniqueness of their own and other families.

Step 5: Closing Celebration

Have the group stand in a circle and sing, "He's Got the Whole World in His Hands." After the first verse, begin to sing the song especially for each family in your group; thus, "He's got the Jones family in his hands," or if your group is large, "He's got the Jones and Smith families in his hands." (If your group is "free" enough, have the families go into the center of the circle and hug or dance around while their verse is being sung.) End with a closing prayer, thanking God for the various families and backgrounds; or ask members of the group to say for what they wish to thank God.

ADDITIONAL PROGRAM IDEAS

The Drawing Game

The game is similar to charades, but pictures and sketches replace motions and sign language. The group is divided into teams. The leader prepares a list of ten words or phrases in advance. One member from each team is given the top item on the list. Then he or she goes back to one's team to draw the word (using no letters or numbers, no sign language, and no talking except to answer yes or no) until someone guesses the item. Another team member then reports the word to the leader, receives the second item, and the game continues until one team figures out all the items on the list. (If your group is anything like ours, you had better have an extra list or two ready.) Play the game either at the beginning of the program as a warm-up or after Step 4 before the closing.

Procedure

Step 1: Divide into groups of about six, keeping parents and junior highs mixed together. Provide each group with lots of scrap paper and pencils, and explain the rules.

Step 2: Begin the game. Here are some suggestions for a list with items that relate to this program.

Family
Thanksgiving Dinner
England
The Exodus
Roots
Grandmother
Atlanta, Georgia
Mayflower
American Indian
Abraham

(Most teams quickly figure out ways to draw even the hardest items and even long phrases. You may want to start with an easy list and then make the items more complicated.)

WHY?

Games are fun, of course, but this one in particular may be able to get junior highs and their parents working together more closely and enjoying one another more. Games should always be included in programs for junior highs; if they can somehow be connected to the theme of the program, they may be even more effective.

A Family Tradition

If you are going to use this idea, it should be placed after Step 4 before the closing of the program.

Step 1: The leader should state something to the following effect:

"One of the values of being more aware of our roots is that we can try to recover some of the traditions we may have lost. We would like each family to meet again and try to figure out someone in your extended family whom you could ask about your family traditions. For example, you might ask a great aunt what her favorite holiday was as a child and what her family did to celebrate."

Each family should decide:

a. Whom you will ask,

b. Who will be responsible for making the contact,

c. When your family should sit down together to discuss what you found out and how you might want to build that tradition into your family's life.

WHY?

This exercise could help families integrate the learning from this program into their lives. Having them decide the specifics of who will ask whom will make follow-through more likely.

Step 2: Have each family report back to the group what it decided to do.

WHY?

Sharing intentions with others increases the likelihood that the family will follow through on its plans and may give another family other ideas that it could use.

Step 3: If you are having another program in a series, have families report to the group the results of their questions.

Rev. Kenneth C. Whitt is the joint program associate for People's and Phillips Memorial Baptist Churches, Cranston, Rhode Island, with special responsibilities for the educational program and family ministries.

LIFE-STYLE

it's all at your fingertips

INVOLVING YOUTH IN COMMUNITY AFFAIRS (TWO SESSIONS)

Delino M. Eslinger and
David W. Swink

WHY?

The great commandment for all Christians is to love—first God, then their fellow human beings (Matthew 22:37-39). *How* to express that love is complicated and sometimes hard to grasp for those of all ages. However, becoming involved in the needs of one's community is one way to practice that love—to feed the hungry, give drink to the thirsty, and to clothe the naked (Matthew 25:34-40).

This program is designed to bring community needs to the attention of junior high youth. These needs directly or indirectly affect the life of the community and consequently affect young people, too. Once they become aware of needs, it is easier for young people to consider an appropriate response.

Adults can become a part of this process by providing a different perspective on community issues. This can be done by adults sharing their knowledge and providing access to the wider community through their friends, acquaintances, and skills.

SESSION I
AWARENESS: YOU AND YOUR COMMUNITY

I. Personal-Need Awareness (20-30 minutes)

GOAL

For each junior high student (and adult counselor) to become more sensitive to his or her personal needs.

WHY?

It is difficult to help others unless one is aware of one's personal needs.

PREPARATION

Adults need to be sensitive to the needs they share with young people. While honesty is significant, the issues involving these needs should not overpower the junior high person.

Materials needed include newsprint, crayons, writing paper, and pencils.

PROCEDURE

Have each individual list personal needs he or she might have—for example, friendship, peer group conformity, physical development, mobility, financial resources, better parental relationships, etc.

Share the lists in groups of three to five people (a counselor may be necessary in each group for a productive session). Have the groups record the needs on newsprint.

Have members of the total group share their new lists and make one list which includes all needs. Have the group reflect and comment on the list of personal needs.

II. Community-Need Awareness (45-60 minutes)

GOAL

To identify as many community needs as possible in a manner specific enough for them to be manageable and understood by the group.

Bad Example: The people in our nursing homes are lonely (too general—problem/need is overwhelming).

Manageable, Specific Example: Sixty percent of the residents at nearby Lakeview Home have no visitors during the year. (One can do something about this.)

WHY?

When young people know of a specific need, they will be more willing (and able) to respond in a helpful way.

PREPARATION

The leaders will want to have collected various resources which will be used in this exercise. These could include newspapers; census reports; magazines, sociological reports; community information pamphlets; significant persons, such as a school principal, police, a county extension agent, a Red Cross worker, a social worker, clergy, a banker, a doctor, etc.

PROCEDURE

Divide into small groups for the purpose of identifying community needs by (a) reading the newspaper or other written material and (b) personal interviews with the resource persons. In the research and interviews, attempt to specify those needs as they relate to your area. Be as specific as possible (see example above). For example: What is the unemployment level in your area? How is poverty defined in your area? Who are the handicapped in your town? In what way(s) are they handicapped— physically, financially, emotionally, spiritually? What are some of the barriers in your community—race, ethnic makeup, labor/management, class structure? (See "Additional Program Ideas.") Have each group record the findings on newsprint for the purpose of reporting to the total group.

Allow each group to report and explain its findings to the total group.

This concludes Session I. In Session II the group members will develop a method for responding to the needs they have identified.

SESSION II
AWARENESS: ENERGIZING FOR ACTION
GOALS

To enable the junior high group to decide upon an appropriate community need and to develop a strategy for helping meet the need.

WHY?

The presupposition stated above, that junior highs will want to help if the need is manageable and specific, applies to this session, also. The task for this program is to develop a manageable, specific community action project for the group to "buy into." When young people are able to see clearly the needs around them, they will have achieved significant growth and will provide the community with aware and active citizens. These benefits are desirable for both the community and the young people.

PREPARATION

Materials include newsprint lists from the previous session, blank newsprint and crayons, paper, and pencils.

PROCEDURE

Have each person take one of the needs expressed on the personal awareness list and one on the community awareness list (from last session) and combine the two through some form of creative expression: poetry, short paragraphs, drawings, etc.

For example: One of the needs expressed by the junior highs might be for a close friend who would be able to keep a confidence, and one of the community needs might be for persons who will visit the Lakeview Home residents who never have visitors. With this exercise the junior highs would combine these two needs, pointing out the similarities and/or differences in them.

When the above is completed, have the junior highs form groups of three to five and share their thoughts with one another. (20 minutes)

In the total group develop a list of community needs in order of their importance to the group. That is, by group consensus decide upon the most pressing community need which can be addressed by the junior highs. Be sure the majority of the group agrees with the choices which are written down! Personal concern for the selected project will bring a higher level of commitment on the part of the group. Also, unless your group is highly unusual, a short-term project is preferable to one which requires a long-term commitment. Most junior highs are not yet ready or able to make a long-term, weekly, or monthly commitment to the community. (20 minutes)

Divide the total group into small groups. Assign specific tasks which will help them grasp the community action project. *(a)* One group can be working on details: date, time, method of transportation, whom to contact, how much money is to be involved, fund raising, etc. *(b)* One group can be working on exploring the nature of the people whose needs you have decided to meet. For example: What are people in Lakeview Home like? What do they look like? What are some of the physical problems they have? What life experience did they have (the depression, World War I, World War II)? Where are their families, etc.? *(c)* Another task group can work on exploring biblical principles, using Ephesians 4; 1 Corinthians 13; 1 John 3:11-18; Matthew 25:34-40; or other appropriate Scripture to develop a rationale for Christian involvement in the community. Include not only why but also with what attitude and spirit the needs should be met. (25 minutes)

Have task groups report to the total group. This is the time when the specific "how to" and "why" will be developed by the group. Here the group will finalize its plans for its community action project. This step will help the group become aware that as a youth group it does have resources at its disposal and will be a challenge for action. By their own research and definition the community action project will be a specific task which is manageable by a junior high youth group. Before you actually begin your project, you may want to consider doing in another session the role play which is found in "Additional Program Ideas," along with finalizing the plans for your project.

WHY?

Junior highs need to have some specific preparation before entering into a new situation. Often their experience has not provided them with the adequate emotional makeup with which to respond to new and perhaps threatening situations.

ADDITIONAL PROGRAM IDEAS

Role Play: Another session could include a role play where the junior highs assume the "roles" of the people who will be involved in the community action project. The purpose of the role play would be to focus on attitudes and feelings of the participants and recipients. Set up two or three possible situations involving the personalities and problems the youth might meet. Dynamics to watch for might include personal fear, feelings of inadequacy, withdrawal, frustration, paternalism, and attitudes of "We're better than you" and "I'm doing this because it makes me feel good" (Do I get involved because it "makes me feel good"? What happens to my involvement if I don't "feel good"?).

For example: When visiting Lakeview Home, how will the group deal with talking to the hard of hearing and the bedridden, strange smells, new behavioral patterns, the obvious effects of aging, etc.?

Allow plenty of time for discussion so that youth can express as many of their feelings as possible.

POSSIBLE COMMUNITY ACTION PROJECTS

Political Action

What area(s) can the group identify where they can implement change in a community? For example: There is not adequate park/play area in your community. With proper research and documentation of the needs, this matter could be brought to the city council for action. (This recently occurred in the Detroit area, thanks to young people of that particular community. It was thought to be an impossible issue by the adults, but the young people succeeded.)

Educational Action

The school system is not providing adequate educational, athletic, or musical programs. Since it directly affects them, what could your youth do?

Social Action

There are families in your locale who are not receiving adequate food/nutritional supplies.

There is a part of the population in your area who are homebound, thus unable to obtain for themselves food, medical care, or other basic services.

The community (including the school) is divided by ethnic, racial, and class barriers, with one group dominating the others.

Church Action

The church could become more active as a center for additional projects beyond what it is already doing.

The local church/churches are weak or totally ignoring the matter of community values. For example: The church is a part of the community barrier problem.

Community Action

The parks, playgrounds, and streets of the community are littered.

With adult guidance and supervision the young people can be challenged to discover and utilize their own creativity and resources to deal with problem areas.

RESOURCES

A Cipher in the Snow, American Baptist Films, American Baptist Churches of the U.S.A., Valley Forge, PA 19481.

Alinsky, Saul D., *Rules for Radicals.* New York: Random House, Inc., 1971.

Keith-Lucas, Alan, *This Difficult Business of Helping.* Atlanta, Ga.: John Knox Press, 1965.

Delino M. Eslinger is director of Urban Ministries and Leader Development for the American Baptist Churches of Michigan.

David W. Swink is director of Christian education for the First Baptist Church in Birmingham, Michigan.

LIFE-STYLE
toward a Christian response to the world

DEVELOPING RESPONSIBILITY FOR OUR ENVIRONMENT   **Frank M. McAuley, Jr.**

GOAL

To develop an appreciation of and a sense of responsibility for God's creation, our environment.

WHY?

All human beings, especially Christians, need to take time to appreciate God's gifts to us in nature. We also need to realize that it is up to us to preserve those gifts for the future.

PREPARATION

Order *And There Was Morning* (a film by Rolf Forsberg, producer of *Parable* and *Nail)* from Family Films, 14622 Lanark Street, Panorama City, CA 91402; 16 mm, 10 minutes, color, rental—$14.00 (price subject to change).

Obtain one or more copies of Dr. Seuss' book *The Lorax* (New York: Random House, Inc., 1971). Look in the children's section of your public library.

Collect newsprint, felt-tipped markers, magazines, paste, tape, and blindfolds for one-half of your usual group.

Warn the group members in advance that they will be spending some time out-of-doors and to dress accordingly.

PROCEDURE

Gather the group together. Have a short prayer. Stand or sit around a piece of newsprint, and then ask the group, "What is the environment?" Another person should record the responses on the newsprint. Following this question, ask the group a second question, "What does the Bible say we should be doing with the world around us?" Record these answers on newsprint, also. Write short answers—a word or a phrase—and accept all answers. There should be no right or wrong answers at this time. (4-6 minutes)

Without too much movement, have the group be seated to see the film *And There Was Morning*. Do not pause for discussion right now. (10-12 minutes)

Assemble the group outside (the weather is not a big factor—merely dress to fit the time of year). Have the group divide into pairs, and give one blindfold to each pair. One person will be a PARTICIPANT and receive the blindfold; the other will be the GUIDE TO THE WORLD. The GUIDE will blindfold the PARTICIPANT and then lead that person around by the hand telling the PARTICIPANT to touch or smell different objects, to listen to different sounds, or simply to walk and experience the world around him or her, trusting in the GUIDE to see that he or she doesn't get hurt or fall. Reverse the roles after ten to twelve minutes. (20-25 minutes)

Reassemble as a total group and have one person write on the newsprint used earlier the different things that the PARTICIPANTS touched, smelled, felt, heard, or experienced. Call out short phrases quickly. Ask for reactions from the GUIDES, and record them on the newsprint, also. (5-10 minutes)

Have someone read Dr. Seuss' book *The Lorax* to the group and then have one or more other persons read the following Scriptures from *The Living Bible:*

 Genesis 1:1-31
 Genesis 2:15
 Psalm 8:5-9
 Galatians 6:7-10

Close with prayer. (15-20 minutes)

HAVE TWO SESSIONS

This material can be expanded to two sessions in the following way:

Program One: Follow the "Procedure" as delineated above up to the activity involving the book *The Lorax*; then close with prayer.

Program Two: Gather the group together and have three people ready to do a reading of Dr. Seuss' book *The Lorax*; one will be the little boy, one the Lorax, and one the Once-ler.

Divide into groups of three or four to look up the following Scripture passages—Genesis 1:1-31 and 2:15 (noting especially 1:28 and 2:15); Psalm 8:5-9; and Galatians 6:7-10. (Use a modern version like *The Living Bible* or *Good News Bible*.) Have the groups rewrite the verses in their own words (you may want to assign particular verses to each group so that all are included). Have them share their group responses. (15-20 minutes)

Make a worship collage or banner. Using a five-foot piece of newsprint, have the total group make a collage or banner of what it has seen and done in these two sessions. Remind yourselves of the film, *The Lorax,* the Scripture verses, PARTICIPANT and GUIDE roles, etc. (15 minutes)

Close with worship. Include the collage or banner and newsprint responses. Sing "For the Beauty of the Earth" or any similar song about creation or the world around us. Have a litany of love: Invite members of the group to call out individually items from the collage or banner or the Scripture or movie, such as "Help me to be like the Lorax!" or "Help us to stop pollution!" or "Thank you for the earth!" or "Thank you for the birds!" Follow each item with the response "Help us to love the world as you do, Lord!" in unison. End with "Amen."

Rev. Frank M. McAuley, Jr., is the pastor of the First Baptist Church, Churdan, Iowa.

ADDITIONAL PROGRAM IDEAS
ADDITIONAL PROGRAM IDEAS
ADDITIONAL PROGRAM IDEAS

ADDITIONAL PROGRAM IDEAS

ADDITIONAL PROGRAM IDEAS

critical first minutes: joy is a key

Duane L. Sisson

Nothing can be colder than walking into a room where a youth meeting is going to be held—especially if you are in junior high school. Those first minutes are very important and can significantly affect the whole program if they are carefully planned.

How can we warm up and tune in the people who enter the physical place of our activities? How do we move them from fear or mistrust and self-consciousness to the positive possibilities before them?

Here are some general ideas to develop to fit your needs. Make them fit your uniqueness; make them fun, energetic, and creative. Work on experiences which include everyone so that a person can easily move into the action and feel the challenge, energy, and fun of it. If in the first moments persons can experience joy, then trust will develop that will enable them to enter into the rest of the activities openly and as themselves. That kind of comfortableness is needed for junior highs and can lead to very meaningful meetings. The first few minutes are critical in achieving this.

It is said very often, but never underestimate it—*prepare the physical place.* Even the smallest changes show concern and readiness. Pictures, color, room arrangement, smells, sounds—doing something with any of these will say right off, "Hey, something is happening here and we are ready to go."

Games are always a lot of fun and catch up junior highs immediately. Charades, hiding an object in the room, guessing which object in the room another person has picked out, imaginary fall, and "Hot Potato" are all games people can join in as they come in the door and which can be ended easily when you want to move on with your program.

Storytelling or sharing is another fine opening experience. You can open by letting someone tell about some experience he or she had in the past week. Not everyone has to share, and no one should be pressured to do so. Listening to the real-life situations other

people experience can be a very active and inclusive event. Sometimes this is hard to cut off, but it can become one of the most profound experiences of a group.

Questions are in the same vein but a little more directive. As persons arrive, they can be given questions, either written or oral. These may deal with the theme of the meeting or just be general interest questions about the persons and what they feel is important. They may talk about them, write about them, draw, make a collage, look up answers, try to guess answers, etc. One can make any number of uses of this method.

Music is a great medium for warming up. It may be simply background music or something more directed. You may ask the participants to listen for themes, people, words, and emotions in a song. You might ask them to respond to a song by means of painting, writing, talking. You can ask them to finish a song or to guess how it ends. You can use their favorite music, or you might use some completely different music to see the reaction to it.

Puzzles are fun; putting together the old-fashioned jigsaw puzzle or building your own can be a relaxing opener. You can hand out crossword puzzles, or the whole group can do one large one. You can make up story puzzles which people need to complete or solve the mystery in it. You can make the persons themselves be pieces of a puzzle and let them put it together. The ways you can use puzzles are innumerable; try them!

A picture is worth a thousand words. Pictures are fun. Whether they are from magazines, photographs, or curriculum, you can study them, arrange them, copy them, discuss them, etc. They are a great tool in programs and also for those critical first minutes. Have them on the wall so that people can look at them or answer questions about them as they arrive. Or have the early youth thumb through magazines to help you find some pictures for the evening's program. Pictures can open people up and draw them into the circle of events.

Crafts, handwork, art projects, or whatever you want to call it can work with any age. Take clumps of clay and have them ready when junior highs walk into a room. Invite the youth to do a particular thing which fits in with the evening's theme or to do whatever they want. You will see a therapeutic and engaging experience. Painting, finger painting, junk collages, craft stick building, paper folding, on and on—any of these media are great openers for your meeting. People have fun with them and become less self-conscious, especially if there are no "right" or "wrong" products and all contributions are appreciated. Discovery is unlimited for them and the leaders.

These are some suggestions. It is hoped they will stimulate many more in your own mind. The Bible and most program themes can be used well with any of them, and all may help you enter into your session with joy, fun, and relaxed acceptance of what you are trying to accomplish.

Duane L. Sisson is an associate minister of the Lakeshore Avenue Baptist Church, Oakland, California, with special responsibilities in education.

ADDITIONAL PROGRAM IDEAS

music ideas

Carolyn J. Mobely

There are so many different ways of using music that this article will hardly be exhaustive. There are musical games which can add life to any junior high gathering, musical productions written just for this age group, and a host of other innovative and exciting music to add sparkle to a junior high singspiration. What I hope to do is share a few ideas or idea combinations that you may not have tried yet. Some of these ideas will be just for fun. Others will be more for learning, sharing, or developing some particular area of Christian life; but I hope they will all be fun to do.

MUSIC AND THE GROUP

Music is the life of any party, including a regular meeting. It can quicken a dying group, excite an apathetic group, and unite a splitting group. In order to advance these ends, the music used must be an expression of those persons involved. Music becomes an expression of the group by identification or by direct creation.

There is an abundance of contemporary Christian and popular music with which young people identify. No doubt you are already using some of it. How often do you write your own songs? Young people should be encouraged to create their own music, at least in part. I know there are not many junior high musical geniuses going around composing original tunes and lyrics. Well, don't start with a full composition. Start with an existing tune that your group knows and likes; then write a new set of words. I think you might be surprised at the genius of many junior high young people when it comes to substituting new lyrics to a familiar tune.

FOR A CHANGE

Challenge your group to rewrite the words to

traditional hymns of the church using nonsexist language. This can be done by individuals or in small groups; then the new lyrics can be sung by the whole group at some designated time. It is amazing how this simple activity increases each person's awareness of sexism in the church and the need for change. The doxology is a good place to begin:

> Praise God, from whom all blessings flow;
> Praise Him, all creatures here below;
> Praise Him above, ye heavenly host;
> Praise Father, Son, and Holy Ghost.

One might render it this way:

> Praise God, from whom all blessings flow;
> Praise God, all creatures here below;
> Praise God above, ye heavenly host;
> Praise Creator, Christ, and Holy Ghost.

Even a hymn like "In Christ There Is No East or West,"* which seeks to communicate the inclusive nature of the church as Christ's body in the world, fails to do so at the point of exclusive, sexist language (substitute words are in parentheses):

> In Christ there is no East or West,
> In him (Christ) no South or North;
> But one great fellowship (family) of love
> Throughout the whole wide earth.

> In him (Christ) shall true hearts everywhere
> Their high communion find;
> His (God's) service is the golden cord,
> Close binding all mankind (humankind).

If verse three is retained:

> Join hands, then, brothers of the faith,
> Whate'er your race may be;
> Who serves my Father as a son
> Is surely kin to me.

*Reprinted by permission of the American Tract Society, Oradell, N.J.

Then a verse like this one is needed for balance:

> Join hands, too, sisters of the faith,
> Whate'er your race may be;
> Who serves the Mother as Her Child
> Is surely kin to me.

Both of these verses become unnecessary when verse three is made inclusive:

> Join hands, then, followers of the Way,
> Whate'er your race may be;
> Who serves the Master as a child
> Is surely kin to me.

> In Christ now meet both East and West,
> In him (Christ) meet South and North;
> All Christly souls are one in him (indeed)
> Throughout the whole wide earth.

This activity might be an excellent prelude to a planned discussion of the issue of sexism in general. If used as a primer for discussion, ten minutes should be sufficient for several small groups to work on the same song, then reunite to share their thoughts. On the other hand, if this issue is of great interest, the group may wish to spend an entire session rewriting a number of songs for use in a special nonsexist worship experience. A group effort to communicate a basic idea or conviction like this serves to unite a group by deepening the relationships within it. The sky is the limit.

PRESERVING GROUP HISTORY

Music is a continuing form of oral tradition. By setting to music the story of an individual or group experience, one can pass on something of that experience to others or simply keep alive the memory of that experience within the group. Unless your group is blessed with an unusually gifted young songwriter, I suggest that you use a familiar tune. This can be a favorite hymn, a tune from a musical you've done, or even a show tune.

For instance, if the group or a significant portion of the group has shared some common experience like camp, a retreat, a conference or youth rally, then encourage the members to put together a song about that experience. If there is a song that was a special part of the group experience, then suggest that tune for the new song. Junior high boys and girls may find the simplicity of a spiritual an easy tune with which to begin.

Try these words to the tune of "Swing Low, Sweet Chariot." This song might be representative of a typical summer camp experience.

> Chorus: Camp time is a great time,
> A time to learn and grow and have fun.
> Camp time is a great time,
> A time to learn and grow and have fun.

> You can meet some nice folks and get to
> know them well,
> A time to learn and grow and have fun.
> You can make some nice things that look
> good enough to sell,
> A time to learn and grow and have fun.

> Well, we had some time to swim, and we
> learned to canoe,
> A time to learn and grow and have fun.

> We hiked up to the mountaintop and rode a
> horse or two,
> A time to learn and grow and have fun.

> We spent some time in prayer just a-talking
> with the Lord,
> A time to learn and grow and have fun.
> We sang a lot of songs, and we read from
> God's Word,
> A time to learn and grow and have fun.

> Chorus: Camp time is a great time,
> A time to learn and grow and have fun.
> Camp time is a great time,
> A time to learn and grow and have fun.

As a group really gets into preserving its unique experience, verses can make specific reference to significant places, persons, and things by name. A song like the one above can be as funny or as serious as the group dictates.

TESTIMONY AND PRAISE

Perhaps one of the most meaningful ways of using music with persons of any age is as a means of expressing praise (love, gratitude, adoration) to God. This can be done testimonially as one seeks to communicate the change in his or her life which came as a result of a personal encounter with the divine. Something as simple as adding verses to a praise chorus like "Alleluia" or "Let's Just Praise the Lord" can have a tremendous impact when it comes from the hearts of those who are singing it at a given time and place. Again, consider writing a new set of words for an existing tune. Try these words to the popular tune of a few years ago, "Bright, Bright Sunshiny Day" ("I can see clearly now . . .").

I can see clearly now the Lord has come,
Bringing new hope and joy into my soul;
God is the reason now for which I live.
This is a bright, bright sunshiny day—yes,
This is a bright, bright sunshiny day.

Look all around—there's nothing but blue sky,
Look straight ahead—there's nothing but blue
   sky.

Christ is the only source of life divine,
Honor and praise are due to that great name;
Glory to God above I'll always sing.
This is a bright, bright sunshiny day;
This is a bright, bright sunshiny day.

The key to success with any of these music ideas is the uniqueness of your youth group. Let the music grow out of its own experiences and interests. This kind of creative use of music increases reflectiveness and thus adds spiritual depth to the corporate experiences of the youth group as well as to the lives of individual young people. It's an ideal way to respond to the love of God in one's life and an exciting way to share the love of God with others.

Carolyn J. Mobely is a home missionary with the Southern Baptist Convention, serving the Atlanta Baptist Association, Atlanta, Georgia, as coordinator of student field work, primarily responsible for the supervision of seminarians doing field work with children and youth in churches and Baptist centers.

ADDITIONAL PROGRAM IDEAS

drama and the church

John H. Duckworth

If someone were to ask me, "What is your greatest frustration in the church today?" my answer would have to be, "The insensitive attitude of Christians and the difficulty of making them once again sensitive to the Scriptures." There are two factors that need to be considered: (1) the Christian of today has heard the Bible stories—for example, the death and resurrection of Jesus—so many times that the individual forgets the original impact the story had for him or her; and (2) because television and movies seem to emphasize violence and cruelty, the individual viewer soon becomes insensitive. The ugliness of the cross and the fascinating resurrection become ho-hum reading compared to the adventures of "The Six Million Dollar Man" or other contemporary superheroes.

How, then, does the church overcome this problem? To become sensitive once again to the Good News of Jesus Christ, we need to make the story more personal and to sense for ourselves the emotion of the story in a fresh way. We need a tool to make us once again aware of what the Scripture conveys. Assuming that we already accept the story as fact and realize its greatness, drama allows us to relive the experience, feeling for ourselves, for example, the emotion of Thomas as he falls to his knees exclaiming, "My Lord and my God!" This tool allows us to imagine ourselves as Thomas, trying to feel what he felt.

Of all the hours of worship I have experienced, very few remain in my memory. I remember as a child sitting in a pew with friends and watching as my mother and father were baptized. I remember, years later, each of my two sisters being baptized. There was action down front, and it was holding my attention. Of course I remember those services in which I was involved and which were extra meaningful to me, such as my being baptized, my own wedding, and so on. Yet personal involvement is not always an important

factor in remembering. Now that I am serving two small churches, I don't always remember those brilliant sermons which I was so proud of when I preached them. I do, however, remember those services in which I could identify with the feelings of the individual about whom I was talking.

We retain more when we have somehow "participated." For example, we may see a preacher and hear him or her; but if he or she stands there like a great oak (solid, unmoving), we may as well sit quietly behind the lady with the big hat. We don't need to look around her to see what is happening; we already know! We can, instead, just sit and listen, trying to concentrate on what is being said. That may or may not be effective. If, on the other hand, this preacher moves around, uses voice inflection, looks alive and excited (as if believing or feeling what he or she is saying), and makes some gestures, then we are interested and will probably go home thinking about what we heard. If one such experience hits home, we may remember it for a long time.

Let's say that our junior high youth group members are putting on a production. It is an improvisation which they have created themselves and have worked hard developing. (An example is included in this article.) Any passage of Scripture is appropriate as long as there is a story to be told and values to be gained. Already the youth have considered the story closely; they must do so if they are going to work with it enough to be able to present it. Now they present it to the congregation. First of all, the audience is hearing and seeing, but there is much more action. If the sanctuary is used, maybe the players can move around among the congregation. Here there might be the sense of touch, also. Add music that the congregation can join in, and you have created a memorable experience for more than just the actors and actresses.

Now break down the congregation into smaller groups, and talk about what was seen and what the present reactions are. Imagine having dramatized Peter's denial: as Peter ran away crying bitterly, maybe some in the congregation knew all too well how Peter felt, as they realized the times they, too, have denied Christ.

There are many variations of this simple formula and many ways that one dramatic presentation can minister to a single church family. Here is a specific example of using improvisation to bring to life a segment of Scripture.

GOAL

The goal of this program is to create in the individual a feeling for the scriptural situation. It is hoped that the individual can identify with the character he or she portrays.

WHY?

One of the biggest problems for any youth leader is to make Scripture relevant to the world today. For example, the story of Daniel in the lions' den seems to be a fairy tale to the junior high reader. In our scientific age such a story seems hard to believe. Furthermore, to realize the faith of Daniel is almost impossible since it often comes across as a story that happened eons ago and, therefore, is not relevant today. When assuming the role of Daniel, two things should happen. (1) The young person playing the part of Daniel becomes aware of Daniel as a complete person. (2) Realizing the conviction of Daniel, the young person is then challenged to live his or her life committed to similar ideas.

Another reason behind using improvisation is the memory factor. Unfortunately, humankind has a great ability to forget. When we use only one of our five senses, we are more likely to forget than if we use all five. In improvisation, we employ sight, hearing (as well as speaking), touch, and, yes, even taste and smell. Participants will remember this experience much longer than last Sunday's sermon even if they are intent listeners.

Another very important reason for improvisation is the opportunity to witness/minister to others.

PREPARATION

Everyone will need a Revised Standard Version of the Bible. For an improvisation use, for example, the third chapter of Daniel.

PROCEDURE

Warm-up Activity (10 minutes)

Have the young people close their eyes and remain quiet for two or three minutes. Then have them imagine the following:
1. Pretend you are in a dungeon.
2. Pretend that it is getting hotter and hotter.
3. Imagine that you see an angel.
4. Pretend that you see the flames all around you, but it is not getting hotter.

Program Content (20 minutes)

1. Read the Scripture passage (the youth should follow along as you read).
2. Assign parts.
3. Go through the passage of Scripture verse by verse, stopping to allow each participant to add creatively to the improvisation as a whole. For example, the group may think that Nebuchadnezzar is an old man. Sally may think that a white wig and beard would creatively suggest his age.
4. Rehearse several times, always encouraging participants to speak loudly and clearly in case they plan to present this to another group at a later time and in case others in that group—who are observing because of shyness, physical handicap, or another reason—cannot hear.
5. Add your own advice as to what seems appropriate or what might give insight to the performers as well as the audience. For example, if you want to let the audience know how hot the fire is, try to show Nebuchadnezzar sweating as he calls the three out of the fire.
6. Refer frequently to the passage of Scripture to be certain that your improvisation is not differing from the original story.
7. Tell them to imagine that they really are the characters they are portraying. How does he or she feel? If a character is angry, then the actor can't be laughing, etc.
8. Have them rehearse it once more with much feeling, keeping true to the characters they portray. Try not to interrupt their rehearsal; write your comments on a separate piece of paper.

CLOSURE EXPERIENCE

1. Have each relate to his or her character: "I would/would not want to be _____." Have each one tell about his or her character in more detail.

2. If you had an audience, ask the people if they believed the characters.

3. Now ask the participants if they would not like to be Shadrach, Meshach, or Abednego; if they say they would not, ask why. If they would like to be Shadrach, Meshach, or Abednego, ask why. The point is that they, like you and me, need to have the faith that those three had. If they don't want to be like Nebuchadnezzar, ask why. Maybe they will answer that he is too wicked/mean/nasty. Zero in on this. Have they ever been bad and felt rotten? How do we as Christians avoid this? You as leader need to be prepared so that whatever direction the discussion takes, you will have some appropriate questions. Think through the group's possible answers ahead of time.

Note: If this group is new, this will help them become better acquainted. If they are old friends, they will have the chance to learn some new things about one another and grow still closer as they realize that the feelings and problems of those around them are much like their own problems, opinions, and feelings.

KEY VERSE

"If it be so, our God whom we serve is able to deliver us from the burning fiery furnace; and he will deliver us out of your hand, O king" (Daniel 3:17).

ADDITIONAL PROGRAM IDEAS

Ask each participant to sit in a circle on the floor and close his or her eyes, thinking of the specific passage of Scripture already used. Then ask each to think of a modern-day situation relevant to the Scripture. Have each of them, in turn, present the situation to the group; then go to someone in the group and carry on a dialogue for about three minutes.

Example

The situation: Your employer plans to fire you if you don't work on Sundays. The dialogue might begin like this:

Participant: I'm a Christian and I don't believe I'm supposed to work on Sundays.

Leader: I want you to work on Sundays; and if you don't, someone else will. You can't just work when it's convenient for you.

Perhaps it will be easier if the leader chooses five or six basic ideas and gets them started. The resources listed could further help you in this area.

RESOURCES (all prices subject to change)

1. C.D.S. Bible Anthology #1, $19.50 plus postage
2. C.D.S. Bible Story #2, $5.95 plus postage
3. Old Testament Bible Squirms, $7.00 plus postage
4. New Testament Bible Squirms, $7.00 plus postage.

Order the above from:
Contemporary Drama Service
Box 457
1131 Warren Avenue
Downers Grove, IL 60515

John H. Duckworth has most recently been acting as interim pastor for the Burke-Lucas Baptist Yoke Parish in Burke and Lucas, South Dakota. He is also the creator, producer, and director of the Montana Religious Repertory Theatre Company, a company of high school students performing religious drama productions.

ADDITIONAL PROGRAM IDEAS

banner making

Susan Kattas

GOAL

To help junior high youth become aware of the rich heritage of art in the church and to help them experience the powerful possibilities of communicating through art.

WHY?

Banners today, as in the medieval churches, are used to teach, communicate, and express the Christian faith and theology. Banners were hung in churches and carried by marching pilgrims as a symbol of victory, victory over death. Their colors inspired and enlightened worshipers in the limestone interiors of medieval cathedrals. The banners created in this project can be a means of sharing a contemporary, individual faith experience, too.

Today most people read, but several hundred years ago the members of a church often could not read and therefore relied on visual symbols to tell Bible stories and to teach the Christian faith. We, too, learn from images which do not involve reading. Examples of these media are television, cartoons, the motion picture, billboards, photographs, and the advertisements and pictures in the many magazines we thumb through. The visual image teaches, communicates, exhorts, expresses, influences, persuades, and enlightens. Religious imagery adds meaning to our reading the Bible, church bulletins, books, and papers.

Because the possibilities are so vast, it will be important for the leader to select a theme that will be limited enough for young persons to complete a banner in an hour yet broad enough to allow each to create a banner that is unique

---

and personal. It would be helpful for a leader to complete a banner before doing it with a group. Going through the project once is immensely valuable in organizing the work space for efficient and productive activity.

Banner making is a commonplace church art activity. However, the usual direction of imagery in design has been verbal rather than symbolic. Printing verses or quotes is a limited way to express oneself when one considers the entire heritage of religious art. The contemporary bumper-sticker-style proclamation of Jesus Christ is not as creative nor imaginative as the Byzantine mosaics or drawings in the catacombs of the early church. Partly, this is the difference between expressing a concept or idea and expressing a feeling or a mood.

PREPARATION

The following materials are needed:

Warm-up: slips of paper
large black felt-tipped pen
simple magazine pictures
masking tape

Banner: felt pieces, 12″ x 60″ of light and dark colors for backgrounds
rod
yarn or rope
felt scraps in a variety of colors
white glue
scissors
pencils
poster with theme and explanations and examples of symbols

PROCEDURE

Warm-up

To stimulate thinking about Christian symbols in art and to get the group warmed up and talking, you may want to use the following game. On slips of paper draw simple line drawings or use magazine cutouts of any Christian signs and symbols (see list below). Tape a symbol to each person's back, and divide the group into pairs. One can ask the other questions about the design which he or she wears, but the answer must be only a yes or a no. See if each one can guess what his or her symbol is—and what it means. Allow up to ten minutes for this activity.

The leader may suggest questions, such as "Can I eat it?" "Is it bigger than my hand?" "Does it walk?" "Does it fly?"

The following are symbols:
Tablets—Old Testament Law, the Ten Commandments
Loaf of bread—Bread, body of Christ
Grapes—Wine, blood of Christ
Peacock—Eternal life, immortality
Shell—Eternal life, immortality
Shaker—Salt, God's people
Lamp—God's people (the light of the world)
Butterfly—Resurrection, new life
Dove—Holy Spirit
Fish—Identification of Christians in the first century
Lamb—Christ
Lily—Purity of Christ's mother
Palm branch—Martyrdom
Vine—Relationship between God and God's people
Fire—Presence of God, Holy Spirit
Rainbow—Union of God and humankind
Nails—Passion of Christ
Ship—Church of Christ
Circle—Eternity, unendingness of God

Banner

Use the lightest and darkest colors of felt for backgrounds because a greater variety of colors will show up in the design. Prior to the activity sew a four-inch hem at the top of each 12″ x 60″ banner. A rod can easily be slid through this hem for a hanger. Attach yarn or rope to both ends of the rod. The wide margin will allow for cutting a pattern in the upper part of the banner, if desired.

Iron the felt if it is wrinkled. If you have to transport the ironed felt, roll it rather than fold it.

Poster with Theme and Explanations and Examples of Symbols

Make a large newsprint poster with the theme, some slogans or phrases related to it, maybe Scripture verses, and a number of symbols which could be used by members of the group in their own banners. This poster is a resource for the participants. The same information could be mimeographed if you don't want to make a poster. Following each word symbol, draw or paste a simple picture. See examples listed above. The goal is to make this a personal experience.

Theme

One theme for a program on banners is GOD, NEIGHBOR, THYSELF, which could be based on the following Scriptures:
Matthew 22:36-39

"Teacher, which is the great commandment in the law?" And he said to him, "You shall love the Lord your God with all your heart, and with all your soul, and all your mind. This is the great and first commandment. And a second is like it, You shall love your neighbor as yourself. On these two commandments depend all the law and the prophets."
John 15:12-13

"This is my commandment, that you love one another as I have loved you. Greater love has no man than this, that a man lay down his life for his friends."

This theme is the central theme of the New Testament. It is the new commandment that was literally carried out in the life of Christ. It can be pointed out that the Greek translation for the word "neighbor" in this passage means the "one nearest you." "One nearest you" may mean near you on different levels, such as physically, emotionally, familially, or circumstantially. How do people love God, love their neighbor, and love themselves? The directive is given in the book of John. As Christ gave his life, so do we give our lives. One may not necessarily give his or her life all at once, as in physical death for a neighbor, but perhaps piece by piece, as in giving life through a kind word, a personal treasure, time, or by giving something which is uniquely part of oneself.

Identify the materials following the explanation of

the theme. Allow each to select a background piece of felt. Encourage them to work their design from the top toward the bottom end of the banner in order to emphasize the elongated format. This is purely a suggestion but is extremely effective. Point out examples of the symbols on the poster.

The leaders may need to help some youth identify what they want to express about themselves. It is possible also to find another Scripture that fits what the individual wants to say about himself or herself. The author of this article designed a dancing figure on a banner to illustrate her appreciation of her jovial nature and sense of humor. The scriptural reference is Proverbs 17:22. The leaders should identify what they appreciate about themselves, for they may want to share this with individuals within the group.

Prepare for a closing. This is very important. Closure in an art activity means showing, performing, or playing the created piece. Perhaps group members will want to display their banners for a Sunday morning worship service, a special church event, or in various rooms of the church for a period of time.

ADDITIONAL PROGRAM IDEAS

The theme for a banner-making activity could be designed around a special event in the church or a camp or retreat. The theme could emerge from a special study, seasonal celebration, or theological concept. The author recommends several work periods for making banners with complex themes.

Susan Kattas is a secondary school teacher from Minneapolis, Minnesota.

ADDITIONAL PROGRAM IDEAS

recreation

Bob L. Rhymer

What do you remember most about your experience in junior high youth fellowship? Is it the Bible studies, the guest speakers, or the worship services that stand out in your mind? For most of us, if we're honest, it's those moments of informal fellowship that we remember best—the leisure-time activities. Our fondest memories whisk us back to that night, after youth fellowship, when we sang ourselves hoarse on the way to the pizza place. A smile parts our lips as we remember the warm atmosphere of Christian friends around the Ping Pong table after evening worship. We almost wish we could turn back the clock as we remember playing volleyball on the beach at the junior high retreat after the morning Bible study. Those "fun times" were pretty important, weren't they? They've stayed with us a long time.

Yet in spite of our own experiences, we don't take recreational activities seriously enough. Many youth advisers see them merely as extras, breaks from the more important aspects of youth fellowship, or gimmicks to insure good attendance. In reality, recreation can be a significant factor in the spiritual pilgrimage of any young person. If handled properly, carefully chosen and planned leisure-time activities provide:

—a constructive use of energy where the pressure of competition is absent;

—an opportunity for the relaxing of tensions faced by all junior high youth;

—an opportunity for youth to socialize in a non-threatening atmosphere, to build relationships with one another (Relationships developed in lighter moments will provide a base for some more serious moments later on.);

—a means by which adults can build rapport with their young people;

—a chance for adult workers to observe their youth as they really are (such involvement allows junior highs to relax and be themselves).

In the first place, junior highs enjoy fun activities and show interest in any group that provides such activities. Although recreation should not be used solely to insure attendance, it must be recognized as necessary for a successful youth program. Junior highs are just beginning the process of being intellectual and logical in their decision making. Thus, a junior high youth will more often than not decide to join a group on the basis of how he or she feels about the group rather than on what he or she thinks can be gained intellectually or spiritually. Attending your junior high fellowship should be fun, and you need not apologize for it.

Secondly, the recreational program can be the fertile soil in which young personalities burst into full bloom. The junior high years begin the long, slow process of self-discovery, and, at times, the pressures of growing up become almost unbearable. In the relaxed atmosphere of fun activities, the young person can escape, for the moment, the pressures of adolescence. The pain of socializing is eased, and walls of separation—such as sex, age, size, and personality—are broken down. The young person can be himself or herself as he or she seeks to discover other selves. The bonds which are built by fun and enjoyment can form a basis for more serious sharing as youth mature.

Finally, the freer and more dynamic atmosphere of lesiure-time activities provides the opportunity for adult workers to build supportive and influential relationships with their youth. Adults who relate to them in this setting find a freer atmosphere and can be out of the usual authoritarian role in which youth see them. In the unguarded moments of a leisure-time activity, adults and youth experience each other as they really are. An authentic relationship often begins on the volleyball court or the trail. And the building of relationships is the doorway to the sharing of deeper experiences.

Getting the proper perspective on recreation isn't enough, however. It will be a positive or negative influence on your youth program depending on how you approach its planning. Following are several guidelines that will help insure that it will be a positive part of your program:

1. Plan activities that most of your group will enjoy, but accept the fact that some may not wish to participate. If there are some who don't want to join in, encourage but don't pressure them.
2. Plan a variety of activities; don't rely on the same old thing all the time.
3. Plan ahead and in detail so that you can relax and take part in the activity. Whenever possible, be a participant rather than merely a spectator.
4. Avoid competitive activities as much as possible. The purpose of recreation should be to build a sense of groupness rather than to divide the group into individuals where some are made to feel inferior to others. For those who want and/or need competition, there are plenty of opportunities elsewhere.
5. Allow your junior highs to plan some of their own activities, even to "dream up" some new ones. This helps to insure more involvement and enthusiasm. The two ideas listed below were "dreamed up" by youth groups.

Huckleberry Finn Outing

For this activity you need food, recreational equipment, a campfire program, several flat-bottom boats or rafts, and a shallow river. Choose a campsite along the river where you can relax and have a campfire program. Have one or two adults transport the food and recreational equipment to the campsite and wait there for the rest of the group to arrive. Transport the boats and the youth group several miles upstream (how far is determined by how long you want to be on the river). After finding a good launching place, the group simply sets itself afloat and allows the boats to drift downstream with the natural flow of the river until the campsite is reached. Then beach your boats and carry out your previously planned program. You might include some games, a hike, a meal, singing, and worship.

Crazy Olympics

This idea is based on the international sports Olympics held in different parts of the world. You can make this program as elaborate as you wish. It is a good idea for an all-day picnic or a weekend retreat. You need some prizes, judges, and a list of Olympic games with the necessary equipment to carry them out. The key to this activity is in your choice of games. The idea is to dream up events that are silly, such as pushing a ball through the grass with your nose, running a race on all fours with your back facing the ground, or carrying a water-filled balloon between your knees to a designated point. The planning committee members will have as much fun planning this one as they and everyone else will have doing it. Any kind of unusual race—the sillier the better—is what makes this a hilariously good time. The prizes can be very simple: candy, combs, key chains, pens, patches, and so forth.

"I came that they may have life, and have it abundantly" (John 10:10b). It was Jesus' intention that we minister to the whole person, his or her social, spiritual, and physical needs. Recreational activities help to meet some of the physical and social needs of your youth, and they help create the group spirit or fellowship necessary for sharing on a more personal and spiritual level at other times. In light of this, how can we treat the planning of leisure-time activities lightly?

Bob L. Rhymer has spent fifteen years working with youth at both local and state levels and is presently serving the First Baptist Church of Newton, Iowa, as its minister of youth.

ADDITIONAL PROGRAM IDEAS

project day—all in one!

Hugh H. Huntley

EVENT: This is an all-day project at the church when as many as five events go on at the same time. These events could be a car wash, a paper drive, a pancake breakfast, a bake sale, and a plant sale. Do as many as your group feels it can take on.

GOAL

This event provides service, raises money, encourages participation, and promotes fellowship and esprit de corps.

WHY?

By concentrating all the efforts of the church junior high team on one event through planning, action, and then celebration, much positive benefit is derived. This intergenerational experience allows for total church participation, with youth doing the work and being visible to the adult church in a creative and helpful way.

PREPARATION

Planning for this event should begin months in advance by getting it on the church calendar and by getting youth and adult helpers to plan for each activity. Perhaps senior highs could help. The best time to have the event is in late spring, on a Saturday around Memorial Day. In most parts of the country this means that the weather is warm and that many people are getting ready for their summer gardens and will be buying "annuals." It means, also, that a churchwide drive to save aluminum and paper can be initiated months ahead of the date, and the good weather encourages people to bring their cans and their paper and aluminum to the church.

Each of the activities should have a couple of junior highs and at least one adult planning and working on it. Publicity can come through the church newsletter as well as through posters around the church and, of course, in the neighborhood stores. If you really want to be energetic, you can run a short ad in the local paper. This usually gets good results.

Here are some suggestions for planning for each activity:

1. Car Wash—Make sure you have plenty of space, at least two hoses or one with a "Y," plenty of clean, soft rags, and special car-washing soap and brushes. Some 3' x 4' posters at the entrance help. Watch out for getting too exuberant—acting silly with water fights takes away from a good atmosphere. The adult in charge must keep order and be on hand to move cars. No youth should drive cars. One person should be treasurer.

2. Paper Drive—Try to arrange to have a local salvage company leave a truck or trailer for the group to fill on that day. Encourage people to bag or tie papers for easy handling, and be sure to check to see if the company will take magazines as well as newspapers. Get drivers to collect *on that day* from those people who cannot bring the papers to the church. Watch out for being used as a garbage collector. Aluminum should be compacted as much as possible and stored in large, heavy-duty, clear plastic bags.

3. Pancake Breakfast—This can be one of the most enjoyable parts of the event in that people come to relax, have a simple breakfast, and participate in the fun at church. Make sure the menu is simple—like juice, coffee, milk, link sausages, pancakes, butter, and syrup. Be sure to organize the kitchen, having cooks, helpers, and a cleanup crew. Many dads love to flip pancakes and to supervise this group.

4. Bake Sale—Here is a much-used service project that

99

has proved to be a success time and again. Many church people can bake even if they cannot get out to participate in any other way. One way to ease the last-minute rush is to plan ahead and put the baked goods in a freezer; just don't forget to get them out at least twenty-four hours before the sale. Remember to have a parent, along with several helpers, work on getting items for the sale well in advance of the day. Plan for an attractive display; put paper on the tables, and supply plastic gloves for handling the food and bags and boxes in which to pack the food items.

5. Plant Sale—This kind of event may be a new idea, but it has proved very successful in many churches. It is especially helpful for older persons who may not be able to get to a nursery for their "bedding plants," such as geraniums, marigolds, impatiens, pansies, asters, snapdragons, and, of course, tomatoes. Many larger nurseries will let you have plants on consignment and let you return those you are not able to sell, taking them back in the afternoon of the same day as the sale. Also, several people in the church may be willing to start cuttings of their favorite houseplants. Again, advance planning is important, with an adult and several junior highs working on and setting up for the sale. Remember that the plants must be attractively displayed, and a big 2' x 3' poster giving the prices should be made. Because of the complicated amounts, it is wise to have a small adding machine or calculator and a responsible person on hand as cashier. See if you can't get a person with the "green thumb"—someone every church has—to be the adviser for this phase of Project Day.

ACTION

Make sure the day of the event is free from other church activities as much as possible. Usually, starting at 9 A.M. with all events makes sense. There will always be the early birds who will be there before the plants are out or before the hoses are set up for the car wash; but 9 A.M., or possibly 8:30 A.M., is early enough. The event's main coordinator should not have to be in charge of any one separate sale but, along with the junior high president, should be checking all of the activities. Each group should have a separate cash bag or box with change in it. The cash proceeds should be gathered at about noon and then again at closing time. All participants should be encouraged to bring their lunches or to eat late pancake breakfasts. Usually by 3 P.M. there is time for cleanup and celebration.

CELEBRATION

One of the best ways to conclude Project Day is with a potluck supper at someone's home and away from all of the confusion of the day at church. A closing devotional and a report of the money made and experiences had bring the whole event to a satisfying conclusion. An alternative to the supper is to have ice-cream sundaes and punch served out on the church lawn. In either case, the important thing is to celebrate and to express thanks to one another and to God.

EVALUATION

In order to get the most out of Project Day, be sure to evaluate the event as soon as possible. Did you accomplish your goals of service and fund raising? Did everyone do a good job? What would you do differently next time? And, of course—last but not least—what are you going to do with all the money you made, and where are you going to put all the junior highs who want to join the fellowship now that you are really doing something exciting?

Rev. Hugh H. Huntley is the minister of Christian education at the First Baptist Church of Redlands, California.

ADDITIONAL PROGRAM IDEAS
intergenerational programs: no easy task

Kenneth C. Whitt

THE NEED

The junior high years are rough on even the best child-parent relationship. For families that have worked hard at building communication lines in the preteen years, the strength of those lines will be tested as junior high youth struggle with questions of identity and independence. In families where little or no attention has been given to talking and listening, there will be rebellion that at best will be traumatic, maybe ending in a painful silence, or at worst will be explosive, leading to long-lasting harm to the individuals and the relationship.

THE GOSPEL

And so there is a great need for the church to bring the gospel of reconciliation and hope to bear on the relationship between junior highs and their parents. And, I believe, there is a strong motivation on the part of the teenagers and their parents to "come together"— if only we can help break through the barriers of fear. For example, I initially began to think about how our church could do this ministry when, in declaring their dreams for the new year, one of our junior highs stated, "My biggest dream is that my mother will like me more this year." But even as I write this article, this person is too afraid to ask his parents to a program we are planning.

BRINGING THE GOSPEL TO THE NEED

In working to set up an intergenerational program at our church, we have come to some conclusions that may be helpful to you:

Don't be in a hurry. It took a long while to erect the communication barriers, and it will take a long while to knock them down. In our initial discussion, our junior high youth decided, with only one voice of dissent (but a very strong voice), not to do anything with their parents. Take time to talk with groups of youth and parents and as many individuals as possible. Plant your seeds and be persistent in your efforts. Don't get hooked into the feelings of some that it is a hopeless problem. And be prepared to stumble.

Lay a strong foundation in other areas of ministry to families. Some possibilities are:

1. Parent Effectiveness Training (PET). PET provides perspective and techniques that can help parents to break strained communication patterns and deal constructively with family conflicts. The book *Parent Effectiveness Training* by Dr. Thomas Gordon (David McKay Co., Inc., $10.95; price subject to change) should be available at your local bookstore or library. Information about the course and names of local instructors can be obtained from Effectiveness Training Associates, 531 Stevens Avenue, Solana Beach, CA 92075.

2. Marriage Enrichment Programs. Again, the emphasis is on communication, and what the parents learn may spill over into the family. Many denominations sponsor programs in this area. For more information, contact your denominational office on a regional, district, or state level.

3. Intergenerational Church School Classes. In the preteen years, introduce the idea that parents and children can learn together. *Young* children are highly motivated to learn with their parents. Griggs Educational Service (1731 Barcelona St., Livermore, CA 94550) has excellent resources for such a program, including *Generations Learning Together* by Pat and Don Griggs ($5.00). Other

recommended books include *The Family Together* by Sharee and Jack Rogers (Acton House, $4.95) and two books published by Fleming H. Revell Company: *Happiness Is a Family Time Together* and *Happiness Is a Family Walk with God* by Lois Bock and Miji Working, $4.95 each. All prices are subject to change.

4. Family Clusters. Families that grow up in clusters are likely to have learned the skills to deal with the junior high years creatively with a minimum of tension. For information on this family enrichment model, write Dr. Margaret Sawin, Family Clusters, Inc., P.O. Box 18074, Rochester, NY 14618. Also, refer to *Family Cluster Programs* by R. Ted Nutting (Judson Press, $2.95). Price is subject to change.

If even a few parents and teenagers in your church have participated in these experiences, you will probably find it relatively easy to set up events for all members of your junior high group and their parents.

Design your own program to meet the needs of your people. Take into account the present communication level of the junior highs and parents and to what you believe they could respond. Maybe a dinner with a musical production would be the right place for you to start.

Emphasize ACTIVITY that will get junior highs and parents working together. Activity is always the rule for junior highs; but in an intergenerational program, activity, even if only primarily for the fun of doing something together, can be a big step forward. Having fun, laughter, and enjoying one another may at least crack many barriers. (How about a bowling party?)

Plan learning experiences that emphasize common- *ality rather than conflict.* Especially at the beginning, avoid subjects such as the relative merits of alcohol versus marijuana or rock versus classical music. I have a hunch that at the level of basic values, junior highs and their parents have more in common than they usually admit; they just rarely talk about these things. (Editor's note—see the program "Roots and Traditions" in the "Life-Style" section for an example.)

CONCLUSION

Most of us have enough trouble just getting our junior high youth group to function well. Intergenerational programs may seem like a luxury we can scarely afford. On the other hand, they may be the only way to minister to some of the most deeply felt needs of our youth and their parents. The depth of these needs points to both the importance and the difficulty of doing intergenerational programs. If you decide to take this ministry on, expect to work hard; but you can also expect to reach into the lives of the families in extraordinary ways.

Rev. Kenneth C. Whitt is the joint program associate for People's and Phillips Memorial Baptist Churches, Cranston, Rhode Island, with special responsibilities for the educational program and family ministries.

Editor's Note:

A number of programs in this volume have been designed as intergenerational experiences. They include the following:
"2Bs + 2Cs=Failure" (dealing with parental expectations and grades)
"When Is Honesty the Best Policy?"
"When You Fight with Your Parents" (see alternate suggestions)
"Roots and Traditions" (exploring family backgrounds together)
"Project Day— All in One!" (a money-raising suggestion)

ADDITIONAL PROGRAM IDEAS
using this book in creating a retreat

Barbara Middleton

THE RETREAT ITSELF

A retreat can serve many purposes:

—It can help integrate new youth into the group.

—It can promote better relationships among current members of the group. This is always valuable, but your group may have a special need to develop better relationships if it has members from several different schools or if some cliques are developing.

—It can provide an opportunity for more extensive study and spiritual growth in a fun context.

Have your youth help you plan. Their enthusiasm and cooperation will be greater if they can help make some of the decisions. You can have one large committee or several small committees, but an adult should work with each committee. You'll need to choose a theme, develop a schedule, and then fill in the program content. Decide on details pertaining to the meals. Who will cook, set the tables, clean up, and provide the food? Plan transportation and publicity. Do you need a money-raising project to keep the cost down? Take plenty of recreational equipment, from Frisbee and volleyball for outdoor use to table games for use indoors.

Of course, your schedule will depend on the place you choose, the time you have available, and the needs of your group. Here is one possibility:

Friday evening

8:00 Arrival, settling in, announcements

8:30 Group recreation or a light activity with some relationship to the theme. (Your youth will probably be too excited to do much serious thinking at this point. Allow them to "let off steam," and don't frustrate everyone—including yourself—by pushing a serious activity.)

9:30 Devotions or singing, if you wish

9:45 Free time

11:00 Everyone in his or her room

11:30 Lights out

Saturday

8:30 Breakfast

9:00 First session. This can take as much of the morning as you wish. Vary the activities. Start with some light, "warm-up" activities which relate to your theme. Junior highs usually don't like to sit and discuss for long periods of time; so give them a chance to move around. About 10:30 or 11:00, play a game of volleyball. This builds group spirit.

12:00 Lunch

1:00 Second session—remember to vary the activities.

3:00 Free time

5:30 Dinner

6:30 Third session

8:00 Planned recreation, or campfire and singing

11:00 Everyone in his or her room

11:30 Lights out

Sunday

8:30 Breakfast

9:30 Final session and closing worship. (Perhaps the youth will want to share significant things which they gained from the retreat session.)

12:00 Lunch

1:00 Leave for home.

Plan to have a balance between group recreation and free time when youth can do whatever they wish. During the free time, they will probably be with their friends. Because these informal groupings provide a special security for them, time should be given for this kind of getting together. But planned recreation which involves the total group will provide for new relationships to be built, maybe break down some barriers, and enable kids on the edge of the group to be included. Such recreation must be planned ahead of time, but it will be worth it.

SOME POTENTIAL THEMES AND PROGRAMS

Any sequence of three or four programs which fit your theme and the needs of your group can be used. Use all or some of the activities suggested, taking into account how long you think the sessions should be for your group. Consider using the additional activities, the recreational ideas, and the worship ideas in the special time slots planned for them.

A Retreat on Personal Relationships

There are a number of programs on personal relationships in this book. Look them over to see which are appropriate to the needs of your group.

This retreat can use:
"Getting What You Want"
"I Love Me"
"Different Strokes for Different Folks"
"Left Out"

Some alternate activities and ideas might be found in
"Ouch!"
"Magic Broom—or I'm In, You're Out"
"Beauty or the Beast?"

The first step is to read through these programs completely, considering all the activities, including the alternate ones. Determine which might be most meaningful for the members of your group. Also, consider the materials needed and the recreational ideas. Here is one possible sequence.

Saturday morning. Use "Getting What You Want." (If the youth are slow in starting, sing some songs or play a brief, active game.) Use the three exercises, reserving the worship for later.

Saturday afternoon. Use a combination of "I Love Me" and "Different Strokes for Different Folks." Use the first three steps from "I Love Me," perhaps omitting the second part of Step 3. Use the first three steps from "Different Strokes for Different Folks," perhaps omitting the role play. These are short and will go quickly. Save Step 4 for later. If your group members are young and you feel that this is too much for an afternoon session, consider saving some of the activities for the evening session or omitting them altogether.

Saturday evening. Use material from "Left Out." Use the game and role plays and the discussion questions for both.

Sunday morning. Allow the youth to react to the activities of Saturday. Let them express their reactions in a collage, a poem, or a favorite piece of music. Use these experiences to create a closing worship. Consider also using the Scriptures and poems in the sessions mentioned above.

A Retreat on Spiritual Growth

This retreat can use the following programs:
"I Am What I Am—God"
"How Do You Relate to Someone Who Lived 2000 Years Ago?"
"Having Supper with Jesus"

The first step is to read through these programs completely and consider all the activities, including the alternate ones. Determine which might be most meaningful for the members of your group. Also, consider the materials needed and the recreational ideas. Here is one possible sequence.

Friday night. Use the "Ring on a String" game in "I Am What I Am—God."

Saturday morning. Begin with Step 2 of that program and continue with the program through the morning.

Saturday afternoon. Use the program ideas in "How Do You Relate to Someone Who Lived 2000 Years Ago?" perhaps postponing the closing until evening.

Saturday evening. Use some of the additional program ideas, such as a faith history or a faith graph. End with the closing.

Sunday morning. Use "Having Supper with Jesus," allowing the first part of the morning to be preparation time. Youth can consider their roles and prepare the room and a very light meal. Have the meal around 11 A.M.

This is a serious retreat and would be most appropriate for a mature group. For a group of mostly seventh graders or youth less involved in the church, shorten the sessions and add more recreation. Planned recreation pays dividends in improved relationships and fellowship.

LEADERSHIP HELPS
LEADERSHIP HELPS
LEADERSHIP HELPS

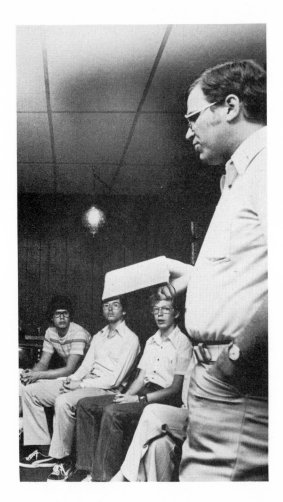

LEADERSHIP HELPS

LEADERSHIP HELPS

the theological basis for youth ministry

Margaret Ann Cowden

As a youth counselor, you stand at one of the first major crossroads in the faith journey of a child of God. That makes you a pretty special person in the lives of your youth. They will look carefully to determine which roads you have taken and why you are now pointing them down one road as opposed to another. Perhaps even more importantly, *you* need to determine the basis for your leadership. Are you adhering to the pattern you think their parents would like to see? Are you motivated by the desire to help others steer clear of the pain you experienced on roads you have taken? While these and other reasons may be well intentioned, they are not a firm foundation for youth ministry. The Word of God is that foundation, and the following insights from it may prove helpful in clarifying your own basis for your ministry with youth.

FAITH IS A JOURNEY

Abraham is typical of the biblical faith journeyer. His story makes it clear to us that faith is no static condition but, rather, a journey demanding all of the skill and energy one can muster. Risk is inherent in the process, but this is a fact of the Christian life that youth will be almost relieved to hear. They are keenly aware of risk in their lives as they move from the relative security of childhood into the rapidly changing, challenging, frustrating world of adolescence. To know that risk and change are not opposed to but, rather, are inherent parts of Christian faith will help in putting those turbulent years in perspective.

If faith is a journey and youth stand at an early crossroad, then great care must be given to the directions they receive there. Pausing at the intersection, bursting with energy like a runner fresh into the race, youth are searching for something to give meaning to life, for sound reasons for following one path as opposed to another. They are ripe for the task of faith building to equip themselves for the journey ahead. Three areas in particular demand their immediate attention, and the Word of God speaks to all three.

ESTABLISHING IDENTITY

"Who am I?"—the question that haunts youth, demanding an answer—has great implications at this crossroad. How can I determine where I am to go if I don't know who I am or from where I have come, what my needs are and how they might be met? Added to the turbulence is alienation from parents, siblings, and even peers, making the struggle seem insurmountable. Developing confidence in their ability to cope with life and to maintain an inner sense of selfhood is a pressing need of youth.

Experiencing anew the reality of being a child of God, with a unique place in the family of God, can help a youth begin to untangle the mixed messages about his or her selfhood. Learning that the emotions that are raging within them are God-given and a part of that creation which God called "good" will go a long way toward helping youth deal with those powerful forces in their lives. They can then begin to listen to the input of their emotional lives, trusting it as one way by which God has equipped them to interact with the world and to provide for the meeting of their needs. They can be helped to see that it is the actions that result from how they handle their feelings, not the feelings themselves, that are subject to affirmation or condemnation. In this way they can be taught to channel the tremendous power for life found within healthy emotional awareness, without either shutting down that vital source of power or falling prey to the whims of emotional extremes. They can then learn how to use this very valuable tool in their relationship with God and with other persons.

Also, to experience anew the transforming love of God is to tap into a tremendous source of healing and growth for teenagers. Exposure to such biblical concepts as God's unconditional love—as evidenced in God's dealings with the people of Israel, as highlighted in the example of Hosea's life, and as demonstrated repeatedly in Christ's encounters with persons—is welcome at a time when teenagers are being barraged with input that says they are anything *but* OK. Being a person whom a loving God has created in love, sought out in love, redeemed by love, and made whole by love is living with a much richer sense of self-worth than adolescents can experience in any human relationships. But let me be quick to add that that love is only experienced as it is mediated by others whose human relationships radiate the presence of God in their lives.

In light of this, your role as a youth counselor gives you the joy and the challenge of helping call forth that very best person God has created each youth to be. There is no finer model of this ministry than the example of Jesus Christ, who could look at the prostitute, the tax collector, the thief, or the leper and see a person of beauty and worth. We dare not neglect this important facet of ministry if we are serious about communicating the gospel of Jesus Christ to youth.

A further contribution that ministry with youth can offer during the painful process of establishing identity is a sense of being a person with a heritage. This is sadly lacking in the experience of most youth today. A mobile society has robbed them of family and community traditions and customs which help to build a heritage. Without that valuable information, youth struggle to understand the context of their own lives and to find models other than parents to help in their own identity formation. A ministry with youth should help them explore what it means to be a part of the people of God.

If this is done, the Bible can take on new meaning for them; it is no longer the record of a people far removed from youth of today. Now it is the record of their heritage as children of God, as twentieth-century members of the family of God, as contemporary links in the people of God. Moses, the liberator, then becomes their ancestor; and Abraham and Sarah number among their parents in the faith. The Bible is no longer a document far removed from their own existence; it takes on a new meaning as the introduction to their own spiritual journey.

In addition, the church takes on new meaning. It is no longer merely a gathering of fallible people but, rather, it is the family of God in which they will grow and live out their faith. It is the context in which they will come to understand what it means to be a child of God with a place and a function in God's eternal purposes.

ESTABLISHING RELATIONSHIPS

Just as the Word of God gives direction on how one develops a sense of personal identity, it also guides one in developing a healthy sense of identity with others. Upon learning that to be a child of God is to be a part of the people of God, youth involved in vital youth ministry soon discover that being the people of God means being a people both of special privilege and of special responsibility. This crucial theme of the Old Testament, one never fully grasped by the people of Israel, will help youth establish a healthy balance in meeting their own needs and the needs of others in their relationships.

Teenagers yearn for deep and fulfilling involvement and intimacy with peers; yet they suffer so in the process of becoming vulnerable to others. To learn the fine art of establishing relationships that are friendly, warm, spontaneous, open, and mutually freeing and fulfilling is to learn an invaluable lesson at an important stage in life. To learn the biblical guidelines for unconditional, selfless, and even sacrificial loving is to acquire an important piece in the puzzle of interpersonal relationships.

One of the richest themes of the Christian faith, that of the covenant relationship between God and the people of God, offers a wealth of insight into healthy relating. Youth ministry that seeks to meet the deepest needs of youth should teach them to build a covenant community. Simply stated, this is a group of people bound to one another by their entering into a mutual covenant which clearly outlines their expectations of one another. It is entered into with the understanding that all parties are to remain faithful to that covenant relationship.

A careful reading of the Bible shows it to be built around the substructure of a covenant between God and his people. All other themes are interwoven into this basic pattern. The Old Testament dramatically portrays the careful building of that relationship between God and Israel, God's steadfast and faithful keeping of his covenant of love, and Israel's stubborn refusal to live within its guidelines, resulting in continual frustration and suffering. The New Testament reveals Jesus Christ as God's ultimate revelation of his faithfulness to keep his covenantal conditions of love and salvation. Finally, his disciples are instructed to bind themselves to one another in unconditional love and selfless giving, building up the body of Christ to minister to a broken world.

Nothing could be more influential in demonstrating healthy patterns of relating than to offer youth the experience of living, even for a few short years, in the security and stability of a covenant relationship with their peers and, it is hoped, with the church family as a whole. The opportunity to share in the celebration of one another's joy and the bearing of one another's burdens will give them invaluable experience in building sound relationships which assure each person of mutual edification and protection from abuse. It will give them a firm foundation for a sound philosophy of life and a truly moral code of ethics.

ESTABLISHING VALUES

Growing out of their awareness of being children of God and part of the people of God will come the impetus to build a life-style of personal integrity. Efforts to succeed in this are the true testing ground for a sense of personal and relational identity. A faithful response of obedience, gracious concern for others, and responsibility for our lives and the corporate life of the society around us are the natural outgrowth of our deepening relationship with God. Vital youth ministry gives teenagers a sense of direction in implementing the standards and values which are the foundation of the Christian community.

There is no better time than the days of youth to enlist persons in the task of helping usher in the kingdom of God. The idealism and unbounding hope that is so much a part of the experience of youth is fertile soil for the planting of Christian truth. Eager to find something that will consume their endless energy and ability to dream and to create, youth will readily respond to a way of life that offers challenge, meaning, and purpose to last a lifetime.

Adolescent years are the time when basic life patterns become firmer and more indelibly engraved upon the life of an individual. It is important for youth to find people who will help them weigh values and then shape patterns of behavior that are consistent with the values they choose. It is also crucial that someone communicate a means by which they can deal with failure when their actions and values become disconnected.

You are truly a blessing in the life of your youth if you introduce them to the delicate tension between grace and accountability as evidenced in Scripture. Communicating to them that God's grace abounds in their lives to cover all failure—all sinning and missing of the mark—and to free them from crippling and unnecessary guilt is introducing them to the only true source of healing for their lives. Likewise, both reminding them of Paul's continual concern to draw on that grace freely, but at the same time to recognize our accountability not to abuse that freedom or take it lightly, and impressing upon them the costliness of God's grace are maintaining their developing a healthy sense of conscience, so necessary for the maintaining of personal integrity and the building of healthy self-love. In so doing, you offer them the crucial guidelines by which to mark their journey as they follow the call of God into adulthood.

Knowing the theological bases for your own youth ministry is a matter of tremendous importance if you are to be assured that it remains centered in the gospel of Jesus Christ and vital in the lives of youth. Consciously determining that foundation of your work may make the difference between merely offering youth programming that at most entertains and keeps youth in a holding pattern during one of their most exciting growth stages and offering significant youth ministry that results in young adults who continue to lead the people of God closer to the kingdom.

Margaret Ann Cowden is the associate minister of the Cambridge Drive Baptist Church of Goleta, California, with pastoral responsibilities.

LEADERSHIP HELPS

"can anything good come from Nazareth?"

YOUTH MINISTRY IN THE SMALL, RURAL CHURCH   David R. Ray

Jesus grew up in Nazareth—a small, rural town. It was so insignificant that people scoffed at the idea of someone significant coming from there. When we consider the boy Jesus, who amazed the elders in the Jerusalem temple, and the man Jesus, who amazed everyone twenty years later, it would seem that there must have been a pretty effective youth ministry at the Nazareth synagogue. It would have been the rabbi at the local synagogue who helped Jesus learn both the letter and the spirit of the Jewish law and Scriptures. That rabbi may have helped shape the character of the Jesus we worship and follow. There is much we do not know about his early years.

Often the lay people and clergy who serve in the small, rural church feel (or are made to feel) that they are an insignificant minority in the mainstream of American life and the Christian church. Statistically, this is not true. If your church has less than two hundred members, it is in the majority. Most major Protestant denominations report that 50 percent or more of their churches have less than two hundred members. If you live in a community of less than ten thousand people, you are not alone. According to the 1970 U.S. Census statistics, 33.5 percent of Americans live in communities of less than ten thousand, and this percentage is rising.

In light of these statistics, there is an excellent possibility that you, the reader, are part of a small, rural church. I am, and I love it. The church of which I'm the minister in Warwick, Massachusetts, has sixty-five members, and the community has five hundred residents. Youth ministry in this setting, as in any other, has rich possibilities and real problems. In this article I am relating both the possibilities and the problems, as I've experienced them.

SMALL IS BEAUTIFUL!

That is the title of a book by the British economist E. F. Schumacher (New York: Harper Torchbooks, imprint of Harper & Row, Publishers, 1973), which has surprised the book critics by being a very popular and influential book. Its central theme is that society works best in smaller numbers, that bigger is seldom better. After doing youth ministry in many settings, my experience is that youth ministry is more successful (in terms of what happens to youth) when done in smaller numbers. If you are in a small, rural church, you, too, are probably ministering to a small number of young people.

Is the following heresy? If you don't have a crowd of youth, rejoice! With a smaller group your youth ministry can be more personal. You can really address the specific needs and hopes of your five, ten, or fifteen youth. What each person says is heard and is important. Each person can really feel needed. (Each one really is needed.) The more people you have, the more impersonal and complicated things get. The larger the group, the more things like planning, transportation, finances, and programming become headaches. If you want to have flexibility and spontaneity in your youth ministry, it's a lot easier if you aren't ministering to a multitude.

One of the most important functions of a youth ministry is to help young people develop leadership abilities. In both a small group and a small church each person has an opportunity and a responsibility to provide leadership. The larger the group, the greater the risk of having not only those who do but also those who do nothing.

If you have a small group of young people, you have

what larger groups are probably yearning for—intimacy, flexibility, informality, and the opportunity for each person to be important. Jesus said, "For where two or three are gathered in my name, there am I in the midst of them" (Matthew 18:20). I wonder if part of his meaning was that in a small group he felt most at home, that that is where he could be most effective, and that in such a group the gospel could be best preached and his kingdom could be best experienced? Small *is* beautiful!

If you are living and ministering in a rural setting, rejoice! Some may ask, "How can you rejoice when there's nothing to do there?" Others may exclaim, "This place is deader than a doornail!" The small town is dull only when you want it to offer what the city offers. When you want what the city offers (culture, entertainment, shopping, diversity), go to the city and enjoy it. But then look more closely at what you have that the city doesn't have—wilderness, space, slower pace, more informality, opportunity to be more personal, and stability. We often take for granted that for which our city cousins yearn.

Rejoice because you can really know the youth with whom you are working. You probably know their parents and grandparents, brothers and sisters, friends and enemies. You know who's having problems in school or at home, who's going out with whom, and who just had his or her heart broken. By knowing all this, you can better laugh with the youth who is laughing, cry with the youth who is crying, listen to the one who needs to talk, and talk to the one who needs to listen. It's true that in the small town everyone (or almost everyone) knows everyone else's business. But I've found that to be more helpful than harmful.

Rejoice because you have a much better opportunity to have a positive impact on the lives of the young people you care about. In most urban areas there are more opportunities for both mischief and serious trouble, more anonymity to hide in, and more demands on your adolescents' time. No wonder so many parents are coming back to small towns to raise their children!

Rejoice because if there is something that needs to be done, it is a lot easier to mobilize people to do it. If you have opposition, you will know (or can find out) who it is so that you can clear up misunderstandings or work out a compromise. And the problems you perceive generally can be solved or at least you can have an impact upon them.

PROBLEMS

Small is, or can be, beautiful; but when we are doing youth ministry in a small, rural church, there are some problems we run into and some problems we often don't even recognize. One unseen problem is the lack of diversity. The tendency is toward racial, cultural, and economic uniformity. While that may mean less conflict, it also means we lose twice. We lose out on the richness and spice of different traditions and viewpoints. And we lose out on gaining experience and insight on how one lives constructively in a world with all kinds of people. Also, this tendency toward uniformity perpetuates the myths and stereotypes (racial, sexual, etc.) which are destructive as we try to build a truly Christian community and democratic society.

Secondly, in small communities we tend to remain insulated from and unaware of many of the issues and problems of our larger world—the problem of hunger, poverty, energy, racism, and urban decay, to name a few. Followers of Christ are mandated by the gospel to care about issues such as these. Someone has observed that we feel less pain from the starvation of millions than we feel from a sliver in a finger.

A third problem in rural living is that many young people go to school, get a job, get married, and stay right where they grew up without ever considering or exploring the other alternatives. The frequent result is bored, discontented, provincial people. I would prefer to see young people choose to live in a small community after considering other choices than to stay there by default.

A fourth problem which I see in our town in particular is a lack of choice of peer groups to join. In our community a youth pretty much has the choice of being a loner or "rugged individualist," or of conforming to the behavior of the single, predominate group. One standard in this group is that it is "cool" to smoke. Therefore, a high percentage of our youth (compared to national statistics) smoke. This is only one example of the power of a dominant social group in a small town. In a larger community, young people have more choice as to which groups to be part of and which life-style to adopt.

In summary, the biggest problem of rural living is lack of choices—in employment, friends, education, recreation, culture, and styles of life. And that brings us to how we go about doing youth ministry in the small church and small community. How do we, the church, go about helping our young people capitalize on all that is beautiful and positive about rural living and at the same time counter the negatives of living in that environment?

EFFECTIVE YOUTH MINISTRY

The first prerequisite for an effective youth ministry is adult leadership. In your church, is the youth program the minister's job? Is there a lay person who has done it for years? Do you have a new volunteer who's willing to give it a try? Here are the qualities I think are most important in a worker with youth:

1. Someone who loves and respects young people and is loved and respected in return.
2. Someone who cares about the Christian faith and witnesses to it by his or her life, not merely with words.
3. Someone who has a contagious *joi de vivre*, i.e., passion for life.

When these qualities are present, the more usual questions of age, experience, time, and talent are secondary. I would guess that any church which takes itself and its young seriously will have people who fit these criteria.

After you have adult leadership, it is vital to research your community. Answers to the following questions would make your program more pertinent, realistic, and successful: How many churches are there in your area? How many of them have a ministry with youth? With which young people? What kinds of programs do they offer? Is there the possibility of cooperative or ecumenical programs? Are there any particular needs the other groups don't meet or segments of the youth population they don't serve? Are there other youth programs in your community (4-H, YMCA, sports programs, etc.)? Do your schools have any after-school programs or services for adolescents? Do many young people go to neighboring towns or cities for recreation? What are the needs and problems, according to your young people, their friends, and parents? What do the police, social services (if any), and schools tell you is needed in the way of youth services?

The answers should point you in the direction of *which* youth need what you can meet, *what* you need to offer, and *when* to offer it. The answers should help you know how to balance your youth ministry in meeting social, recreational, personal, and spiritual needs.

Potential resources need to be researched. This will help you determine who and what is available to you. What radio station(s) and newspaper(s) serve your community? They will probably give you lots of free publicity and can refer you to other resources. If you like to use newsprint (for murals, table covering, in place of chalkboards, etc.), your local or closest newspaper will probably give you the butt ends of their rolls of newsprint. I got a lifetime supply just by asking once!

Is your elementary or high school willing to share the resources and equipment you can't afford—such as projectors and tape recorders? Through them you might be able to borrow from your state university's film library.

What resources does your public library have besides books? Our regional library system has an excellent film collection, with hundreds of films that are available free.

Your state or regional denominational office probably has an extensive range of books, filmstrips, and possibly films which can be borrowed.

Large sister churches often are happy to loan or give away unused resources. Last week I came back from a Christian education conference with a trunk-load of church school curriculum and the promise of more.

Your local library has crafts books with terrific ideas of things you can make from "junk," and your friends in and out of the church will be happy to deluge you with the requisite junk. You just need to ask.

What *people* resources do you have? There is an abundance of people in your church and community with skills, interests, experience, and lots of love just waiting to be shared (a photographer, a writer, a crafts person, etc.).

Your church building, church property, the homes of youth and church members, the neighborhood, the community and the surrounding area are all resources waiting to be tapped. Last year our youth planted pumpkins behind the church and sold them for a total of almost a hundred dollars in the fall. A tour of the local bank (the vault is a hit) is a good way to start a discussion of the use and abuse of money. A local funeral home tour or gravestone rubbing in the cemetery is a good start for a focus on death and dying. The best nature study I ever saw happened when each person was given a ruler and a magnifying glass and asked to study one square foot of nature for fifteen minutes. Your local environment is an endless resource!

Now that you have leadership and have researched the needs and resources of your community, you are ready for youth ministry. If you have included youth in your researching, you will not have to look for them now. They will be there. Now, what is it that you want to happen when your youth and adults come together? Your youth ministry must be prefaced by some goals and your activities evaluated in light of them. Here are my goals for my ministry with youth:

—I hope our youth learn to like and respect themselves. Our plans should include experiences that will help our youth feel proud, valuable, and worthy. If they do, they will not sell themselves cheaply.

—I want our youth to learn to respect the rights of others—the right to be different, the right to privacy and private property, the right to the things that make life livable. We will have to do things and go places which will encourage identifying with the lives of all kinds of people.

—I hope our youth will discover a purpose or destiny for their lives. We will need to consider present skills and interests and future possibilities for our youth as we program. Being "in the image of God" needs to be understood.

—I want our youth to see enough of the world to feel at home in it. Our activities will have to include opportunities to travel, meet people, and share a great variety of experiences. How can we help them learn that the world is our neighborhood?

—I want our youth to discover they can have an impact, make a difference, leave their signatures on the world. Our program will have to include opportunities to be involved in real problems. Our lengthy involvement with Heifer Project International has helped us feel as if we have really helped hungry people feed themselves.

—I hope through all that we do together, our youth will find the Christian faith to be a source of strength, meaning, and direction. We must include opportunities for encounter with deep questions and for worship and celebration that touch their lives.

These are my goals. What are yours? Jesus said, "For where two or three are gathered in my name, there am I in the midst of them." If you are working on goals such as these, God will be present in your youth ministry, no matter how small your numbers or how remote your location.

David R. Ray is pastor of the Trinitarian Congregational Church in Warwick, Massachusetts, and is in the Doctor of Ministry Program at the Hartford Seminary Foundation, Hartford, Connecticut. He has worked in a variety of youth ministry settings for fifteen years and has made a career commitment to ministry in the small, rural church.

LEADERSHIP HELPS

fiddles, banjos, and guitars: the importance of multicultural life

William Mamoru Shinto

INTRODUCTION

When I was a seminary student pastor, my wife Ernestine and I left urban Louisville and switched settings to rural western Kentucky—the Dry Valley Baptist Church of Mystic. On several Saturday nights, the small community would gather to "make mountain music," and we'd sit back and enjoy such tunes as "Flop-Earred Mule." Among the instruments were the fiddle, the banjo, and the guitar. And therein lies a tale of multicultural life.

In Appalachia and the Ozarks dwell the folk who preserve old ballads and fiddles of the British Isles. Through years of cultural contact with blacks, especially the Afro-American churches, gospel music and the banjo were added. Out of Iberia through the southwestern region of the United States the guitar took a prominent place in country music. Thus, whatever one's racial identity, the resulting music was an enriched, powerful melding of the contributions of each culture into the wholeness of a distinctive American sound.

WHY MULTICULTURAL LIFE?

Multicultural issues center not only on the problems of racism and poverty but also on the long-range responsibility to be culturally enriched by every segment of our diverse society. Whether our concern is the changing ecological conditions of spaceship earth or the enrichment of life through aesthetic enhancement, our nation needs to focus on multicultural opportunities as positive resources for alternative ways of constructing a qualitatively different future.

Historically our nation, often with the support of the churches, has tragically tried to deal with diversity by genocide of the American Indian, enslavement of blacks, colonization of Hispanic and Asian Americans, and "Americanization" to an Anglo-Saxon uniformity through both schools and churches.

However, neither cultural genocide, segregation, nor integration solved problems. Today there is a thrust for cultural pluralism and cross-cultural unity which harbors more hope. The world is indeed an almost infinite variety of cultures, languages, and ethnic groups. Each group can add to the positive changes by providing a variety of solutions and lifestyles through which the problems of the future may be solved.

The churches' participation in multicultural life is essential since churches are a source of values and beliefs which are central to the future. As churches, we need to affirm the diversity of our society while at the same time seek to enhance those commonalities which create wholesomeness in our lives.

The apostle Paul reminds us that "the body does not consist of one member but of many. If the foot should say, 'Because I am not a hand, I do not belong to the body,' that would not make it any less a part of the body. . . . The eye cannot say to the hand, 'I have no need of you,' nor again the head to the feet, 'I have no need of you. . . .' If one member suffers, all suffer together; if one member is honored, all rejoice together" (1 Corinthians 12:14-26). Thus our ministry of reconciliation is not one of changing our brother or sister into our likeness but of knowing and appreciating who he or she is.

This is a massive task, given the fact that our churches, through voluntary affiliation, are basically monolingual and monocultural. But we know that racism and an attitude of white superiority are learned; so they can also be unlearned. Thus the educational processes in our communities, including that of the churches, can either enhance cultural pluralism or continue to repress diversity.

WHY JUNIOR HIGHS?

In studies of growth and development the child goes through three broad stages in emerging cultural attitudes. The first is pregeneralized learning up to the age of six. "Patriotic sociocentricity" emerges first. Group identity (racial, national, religious) increases with age, and one recognizes one's own group before thinking about others. What is learned about other groups is simple, whether they are considered "bad" or "good."

At about age seven or eight, linguistic tags provided by significant adults, including ministers and church school educators, begin to be attached by the child to culturally different groups. Basically these are negative stereotypes which result in viewing variant groups as "all bad."

From twelve years of age the young person begins to make adultlike differentiations; the linguistic labels now have both negative and positive traits. However, the person adopts the stereotypes of adults and the general community. For example, high school students in a survey attributed the "positive" qualities of rhythm, cheerfulness, and music to blacks.

One can then see that the critical junior high years either correct the prejudicial stereotypes of the society or merely reinforce the racism of the society.

RACIAL ISOLATION: A PRIORITY ISSUE

The public issues of black unemployment, bilingual educational needs of Asians and Hispanics, the poverty of most minorities, etc., are very important issues which each junior high group should know. On the other hand, a key issue is often neglected by churches. That is the issue of the racial isolation of the majority.

A superintendent of public schools recently told me of her firm conviction of the value of bilingual education. She lives in a community with few minorities, but has initiated a bilingual Spanish program for both Hispanics and whites. The program is as essential to the growth of the white child as for the Chicano.

Racial isolation is not the primary problem of minorities. It is a priority issue for whites, for the most racially isolated children are white suburban children—precisely those of the families of the majority of our churches. The whole spectrum of the "educational" experience of the child—church, school, community, and family—is critical for the cultural attitudes which will guide a person's entire life.

Furthermore, racial isolation is closely linked in our society to religious isolation. Although mixtures of population no longer make this inevitable, churches are often "segregated" into ethnic and language groups—e.g., Hispanic, Irish, and Italian, Roman Catholics; Jewish temples; Japanese Buddhist temples; Scandinavian and German Lutherans, and a variety of ethnic Protestant churches. Your church might itself be a mixture of ethnic and language groups, especially if one is aware of the rising, new self-identity of white ethnics.

Thus, the twin issues—racial isolation and religious isolation—can become the focus of an imaginative junior high church education program, utilizing the resources found in the community itself—the families, churches, temples, public schools, and libraries.

WHAT ARE EDUCATIONAL MODES FOR CULTURAL LEARNING?

Jerome Bruner stated that any body of knowledge can be represented to the learner in three different ways: the enactive, the iconic, and the symbolic. These may be combined in various ways. Taking a cue from this framework, cultural learning can take place in many ways.

Enactive. This is similar to the familiar "learning by doing" method. One learns about a different culture by "doing the culture." The simplest way is through eating the food, playing their games, observing and studying various aspects of the group. In a multiracial community there may be ethnic schools, businesses, and celebrations, from Cinco de Mayo, black festivals, and Hanukkah to the Chinese New Year and Indian Pow-wows.

In monocultural communities there are fewer resources, but the ideas are no farther away than the library and museum, the public schools and the universities.

There are, to be sure, problems, since any real learning which involves internalizing the values of a culture takes time and depth, such as that experienced by some overseas and domestic mission personnel. The superficiality can be avoided by setting clear goals, such as appreciation for others, rather than by using these experiences for their entertainment value. A dialogue on the meaning of the experience is essential.

Iconic. In this mode of learning the young person is presented with such things as models, graphs, pictures, images, charts, and other kinds of aids. Basically, this learning depends upon the teacher having some understanding of the culture and the purpose of using such aids. The "iconic" forms are used since learning takes place more quickly with such pictorial representations than with mere use of words.

The line is thin between "iconic" and "symbolic." The use of flower arrangements is a case in point. Japanese flower arrangements (one school is "Ikebana") may be learned and used in the churches, becoming an iconic form of instruction. At another level, when studying the history and meaning of the arrangements, they become symbolic.

Symbolic. The thought and expression of the culture is most clearly present in the symbolic mode. Humans are symbol-creating animals, and their thoughts and artistic expressions are symbols of how they perceive and live in the world. These may be novels, plays, poetry, dance, paintings, essays, and religious thought and rituals.

These "symbols" point to both the reality of the variant culture and its mystery. That is, they both reveal the essence of the culture and conceal the depth of it; so no study can completely reveal the meanings; for part of them is always beyond description on the "feeling level." In fact, a person *in* a culture experiences the same paradoxical clarity of meaning and awesomeness of the mystery. When the symbol loses that paradoxical quality, it can no longer be considered a real symbol.

Perhaps an illustration would be more meaningful to you here. In too much of the life of the Protestant churches, there is still a very superficial educational process concerning our relationships with Jews. One important means of learning how to break out of cultural isolation is to have an educational program which takes seriously the fact that Jesus Christ was Jewish and a faithful adherent of the Jewish faith. This immediately places the study out of the strange misinterpretations which misinform our children. Jesus was not a white Protestant; he was a faithful Jew. By the simple method of turning our Easter holiday into Holy Week informed by the Jewish tradition, we would be engaged in very powerful cultural learning and feel the strength of the Jewish religious symbolism. The church could celebrate Passover as did the Hebrews, perhaps even inviting a Jewish family or rabbi to lead it.

That event might then awaken the church to the richness of multicultural, interfaith experiences. A church alive to such multicultural learnings will have a very significant role in shaping the multicultural attitudes of its young people, thus taking them out of their narrow racial isolation.

CONCLUSION

In 1934, two white folklorists, John and Alan Lomax, recorded a dozen blacks in a rural church who danced with a steady rocking beat, singing, "I've gotta rock!" The black churches were one of the carriers of the religious and musical heritage of Africa and their slave experiences here, forming them into a composite cultural force which impinges today on the whole society. The other carrier, interestingly enough, was the black chain gangs.

We have already noted the black impact on country music, but the most important thrust is in rock and roll, the "educator" of every junior higher in the nation. Memphis was the home of the rawest black boogie, and nearby in Tupelo, Mississippi, Elvis Presley was born in 1935. Coming out of the Pentecostal church, Elvis banged out "That's All Right, Mama" in a Memphis studio and changed the course of pop music overnight.

Rock conjures up in adults either hope or vast outrage. One Baptist preacher in Tallahassee, Florida, had his young people set fire to about two thousand dollars' worth of rock records. But rock and roll defines the new generation's sensibility, style of life, and fantasies.

The themes, arising out of the black experiences and the tradition of the religious mountain folk, have deep, symbolic, and human force, very different from the sentimentalism of much which passes now as "modern church music," the old language of Zion set to a beat.

In the most racially isolated town in the nation, the junior higher is moved by rock and roll, which conveys to them a multicultural experience—the blackness of the Afro-American church and culture, the folk tradition of the country folk in the mountains, the strains of Hispanic influence in the singing and wailing guitar. It is an experience in all three modes of learning: enactive, iconic, and symbolic.

It is imperative that the church begins to understand the pervasiveness of the multicultural nature of our society. We might all be much richer as Christians and humans if we could identify and embrace what is already a reality—the blackness, brownness, yellowness, whiteness, redness, Jewishness of our existence, and all the richness of life that that reality implies.

Certainly one could burn the records, but no one can deny the vitality which emerges from the powerful symbols of our life. The leaders of junior highers would do well to recognize the multicultural roots of our daily life, such as rock and roll, and begin a process of dialogue with the young people on the *meaning* of that symbol in their own lives and to the society's future.

RESOURCES

Bruner, Jerome, *Toward a Theory of Instruction*. New York: W. W. Norton & Co., Inc., 1968.

Guralnick, "Elvis Presley," in *The Rolling Stone Illustrated History of Rock and Roll*. New York: Random House, Inc., 1976, pp. 30-34.

Haque, Abdul, "The Learning of Nationality Stereotypes During Childhood," *Topics in Cultural Learning*, August, 1976, pp. 3-5.

Palmer, Robert, "Rock Begins," in *The Rolling Stones Illustrated History of Rock and Roll*. New York: Random House, Inc. 1976, p. 10.

Shinto, William, "Colorful Minorities and the White Majority," *UMHE Monograph*, no. 1. Available from United Ministries in Higher Education, 3 West 29th Street, Suite 708, New York, NY 10001 for $1.00 (price subject to change).

William Mamoru Shinto is on the staff of the United Ministries in Higher Education, New York City, and works with various ethnic caucuses and public education groups.

LEADERSHIP HELPS

the youth on the edge

V. Rex Woods

We all have them: the youth whose names are on our rosters because their parents belong to our churches, but none of them are active in any aspect of our churches' life; the youth whose parents are actively involved in our churches but who are themselves uninterested and uninvolved; the youth who come to our youth groups only sporadically—perhaps to parties, or a retreat, or an occasional meeting; the youth who come because their parents make them come but who, if given their choice, would be elsewhere; youth who want to be a part of things but are shut out by the group; youth who come to meetings but who seem to be strangers to the proceedings. These are the youth on the edge.

If we think of groups as circles with the most active and committed members at the center, then as we move outward through bands of decreasing involvement, we find that these youth are the ones who will be on the edge. They are still within the circle, but they are farthest from the center. The boundaries of the circle are not rigid; people can, and do, move from one level of participation to another. Perhaps with only a slight nudge, these youth on the edge could be brought into the center of the circle—or they could be pushed beyond its boundaries.

Most of us know *who* these fringe youth are, but do we know *how* they got to be that way? It is important that we recognize the process if we are going to relate to them effectively—and it's not likely to be the same for any two youth. One may be moving toward greater participation in the group, needing encouragement and support, while another may be moving away from the center in rebellion, needing patience and understanding and freedom. The youth on the edge could be moving in opposite directions in terms of their relationship to the group and at different rates of speed; so, of course, you will relate to them differently.

How do you find out how the youth have gotten where they are? You will need a healthy sense of curiosity, but chances are that you'll learn more through careful listening and watching than you will through probing. Even if the youth do understand the dynamics of their situation, they may not be able to explain them, and asking them, "Why?" may only put them on the defensive, thereby making them harder to reach and perhaps even pushing them beyond the group. Following are a few of the reasons youth might be on the fringe of your group and some ideas about relating to them in these circumstances.

PERSONAL INSECURITIES

The early years of adolescence are, for many, a time of personal insecurity. Junior highs think of themselves as too old to be regarded as children, but few have the maturity to be considered adults. They are striving for acceptance by their peers, and they become terribly self-conscious about what they say, how they look, and what they do—and especially the effects these will have on the ways their friends will value them.

It could be that simply coping with home and school has drained them emotionally as they try to answer the age-old question "Who am I?" and that they have neither the desire nor the energy to add the complications of another set of relationships to their already difficult task. With such youth you can do several things.

First, you can accept them as they are. But make sure that the acceptance is real and that you're not just *talking about* it; you can bet that the youth will know the difference! Second, you can sympathetically let them know that you recognize their struggles for personal identity. They may not have talked about

117

them with you, but you have surely seen them, and perhaps you have even got caught up in some of them. Let them know that you are committed to working through these difficult times with them.

As an illustration, my son and I seemed to be in almost constant turmoil when he was in his early teens. Finally, one day, in exasperation, I blurted out, "Look, I know how difficult it is for you to be a teenager, but this is my first time as the father of a teenager, and it's hard on me, too!" It didn't solve all our problems, but it did make us partners in the struggle, and that seemed to help. Third, you can help them think about themselves theologically. They are, first, children of God, and accepting this truth could go a long way in helping them with their other relationships.

ASSERTIVENESS

Sometimes, as part of their search for identity, adolescents may become self-assertive—or what some would call "rebellious." Perhaps they grew up in the church; now they may feel that "church school is for kids" and that they have outgrown it. Or they may ask defiantly, "Why do I have to go to church?" That kind of question is sure to get our defenses up! We may feel that they are about to move outside the circle and that we're about to lose them; we may feel threatened. But let's not lose sight of the fact that these are legitimate concerns and questions.

A sensitive counselor can defuse the question by helping youth identify the real issues involved; by going beneath the surface, he or she can then share at a deeply meaningful level with a searching young soul. The youth may be asking what meaning religion can possibly have in his or her life; this becomes a good opportunity for the counselor to share something of his or her faith. Or they may be asking, "When will I be mature enough to make some choices on my own?" Or they could be asking, "Who are the legitimate authorities in my life? My parents, my friends, my church, or myself?" These are all good, searching questions, and the counselor who takes them seriously is building a solid relationship. The questions should not be shirked; for hard questions, honestly dealt with, often become the basis of a mature faith.

Many of our youth will never become openly rebellious, but in countless ways they will show their resistance; they will agree to assume some responsibility but fail to carry it out; they will be mildly disruptive in meetings; they will procrastinate; they will fail to follow directions on some task; their methods are endless! Make no mistake: their behavior

reveals that these questions are implicit in their minds and must be dealt with at some time.

CULTURAL EXPECTATIONS

Community and school expectations play an important—though usually unacknowledged—role in helping youth answer that all-important question, "Who am I?" The expectations are rarely voiced but are most often found in customs or traditions. Some may be positive and some may be negative, but in either case there are subtle pressures to conform to community expectations. From where do the pressures come? From the internal desire not to be different; that desire is rooted in the nature of adolescent behavior.

Different communities have different influences and expectations: some seem to expect that their youth will finish high school, get married, and stay within the community; others seem to encourage their kids to finish college and to settle elsewhere; some seem to expect their kids to experiment with drugs or sex or alcohol; some promote a competitive spirit with a strong emphasis on school athletic programs. The effective youth counselor must recognize these subtle, unseen, and unspoken influences and understand the meanings that they have for the youth in his or her group, even though the youth themselves may not be aware of the significance of them. Such an understanding, in and of itself, can be the basis of a good relationship, for the youth will intuitively sense that here is someone who appreciates their concerns. But youth counselors can go further: they can bring community values into the open with youth, through formal programs or informal discussions, where they can be evaluated and affirmed or rejected.

UNFAMILIAR PROCEEDINGS

Other youth may be on the edge of the group because they feel that they are strangers to its ways. You might think that "all" the youth know "all" the words to at least sixty-three different choruses; but if there is *one* who doesn't know the words, it can—at least in his or her own mind—set him or her apart from the group, keeping him or her on the edge. Help him or her to know the words! Give him or her a songbook or a song sheet, or go over the words before singing them. Or if you're using Bibles for study or discussion, it would probably help him or her if everyone used the same edition so that you could also use page numbers for reference as well as the names of Bible books.

The same kind of thing should be done with prayer. I

once took a group of young people backpacking. Because they were all from our church, I assumed that they were familiar with prayer; so I assigned each one a turn saying grace before meals. The first person chose a silent prayer; the second had everyone join in saying, "God is great, God is good . . ."; and the third shouted, "Rub-a-dub-dub! Thank God for the grub!" I had finally begun to realize that we were headed downhill, and I shuddered when I thought about what "prayer" might be like five days down the line. So for the next meal, I asked each person to name one thing for which he or she could honestly be thankful for that day; they offered such things as "no rain," "eating berries along the trail," "finding this neat campsite" (beside Lake Superior), and "no bears in camp last night" (a real concern!)—and from this we made a litany. We need to do things like this to help people feel comfortable with religious practices and at home in our groups.

POOR FAMILY MODELS

Among the most difficult youth to relate to, in my experience, are those who have poor home models, at least in terms of their relationship to the church. There is no incentive from within the family circle to encourage their participation in our youth groups. Throughout their lives, their family interests have been elsewhere: weekends at the cottage, camping, boating, skiing, family gatherings, etc. Or maybe the parents have been pushing their children into Little League, scouting, swimming lessons, music lessons, or any one of countless other things—but never the church.

To relate to youth in this group, you usually have to meet them on their terms—which is not so unusual itself, except that they are more likely to be further afield from the interests of you and your group. If you are successful in establishing a relationship with them, you may still be a long way from getting them involved in your group; and even if you do interest them in your group, you still have the apathy—and quite possibly even the hostility—of the family members to overcome, for they may feel that their values are being challenged or disrupted. Relating to these youth requires a lot of imagination and perseverance, for their exposure to the church and the Christian faith has often been only casual and superficial.

POOR PROGRAMMING

Finally, some youth are on the edges of our groups by choice, but not necessarily by preference, simply because we have done a poor job of programming. We should not always assume that the youth are on the fringes because of some quirk in their makeup. Some youth may be on the edge because they feel that the programs are too sophisticated for their needs or interests, and there may be others who are on the edge because they find the programs too shallow and simple. In either case, they may be on the edge because they are bored by what the group has to offer.

Is there too much Bible study? Or not enough? Is there too much recreation? Or not enough? Maybe there is too much emphasis on social issues and not enough on personal concerns—or vice versa! Working with adolescents requires considerable flexibility on the part of adult leaders. What may have been acceptable to their brothers and sisters—perhaps even as recently as last year—may not be acceptable to them. Programming with youth is changing.

Some of the changes might be simple: it might be better to meet on Thursday evening or Tuesday after school rather than Sunday evening; perhaps it would be better to meet in homes rather than in the church; maybe three or four weekend retreats a year would be better than weekly meetings. Other changes might be more difficult to manage; but at least give them a try!

So there are six reasons why some of the youth in your group might be on the fringes, though, of course, that number could be multiplied many times over. It is a temptation to pass over these youth in order to concentrate on those who have shown a more serious interest in our groups. This is easy to justify: "If we have better leaders, then we'll have better programs; and if we have better programs, then the youth on the fringes will become interested." That sounds good; there is enough truth in it to make it attractive—but my reading of the youth groups I've known leads me to say that it just isn't necessarily so. I think the fallacy there is that we are putting programming above people. In this case, the people are the youth on the edge, and I suspect that many of them are there in the first place because they haven't been taken seriously as people. So good programming is not the complete answer.

No, I have a hunch that the real battles are fought not at the center but at the edges; there is where the youth are wavering; there is where some crucial decisions and choices are being made. When youth leave our groups, they leave not from the core but from the edges. And when they come into our groups, they come in by way of the edges first. We need to pay attention to these youth, for what we do with them, I suspect, determines the future of our groups.

V. Rex Woods is pastor of the Whiting Community Baptist Church, Neenah, Wisconsin.

LEADERSHIP HELPS
coping with cliques and couples

David L. Silke

We are living with a dilemma in the area of communication. It is troubling that in this period of advanced technology, when a minute of TV time can cost an advertiser a hundred thousand dollars to communicate a commercial message, two people who want to communicate are at a loss as to how to do it. The advertiser spends thousands of dollars to secure the very best methods of communication, while we as individuals lean heavily on our own resources and stumble along trying desperately to communicate by controlling or seeking the attention of those around us in inadequate ways.

This is just what many (if not most) couples and cliques are doing when they become a problem in a group organized for broader purposes, such as study, fellowship, and personal growth. The couple or clique that causes a problem in a group (not all do, of course) is the one that has put its own personal needs in the place of prime importance. That is very human and we have all done it, but every member of a group needs to develop some sense of responsibility for the group(s) to which he or she belongs. Of course, it will be most beneficial if a group can be helped to understand the needs of the temporarily self-centered couple or clique and plan programs and activities to help meet those needs.

We probably have all experienced the couple or clique (a small group of people heavily dependent on one another for the meeting of their interpersonal needs) that can't seem to join fully into the group and recognize that there are others around who would like for them to share some of their life with them.

The couple (two people, not always boy-girl) or the clique will often sit together, perhaps in a corner or on the edge of the group. The use of a circle for discussion and activities will help bring them into the group.

They will focus attention on one another rather than the speaker or leader. The thoughtful and alert leader will seek the attention of the couple or clique through eye contact, proximity (moving closer to them), or by direct verbal confrontation using questions and comments directed to them by name. These questions and comments should never be derisive or embarrassing.

If a problem persists, it is often profitable to have a conversation with the individuals involved. This should be done completely apart from the wider group so that the individuals do not feel embarrassed. The "problem communicators" should never be publicly criticized or embarrassed, as this is almost always counterproductive.

During the conversation with the couple or clique (sometimes only the leaders of a clique need to be confronted), the health and welfare of the wider group should be the focus of attention. Do not tell the offenders what is wrong with them. This will put them on the defensive and cause guilt; rather, encourage them to try their best to provide their interest and ideas to the larger group. Often the support that a small group has been withholding through their cliquishness will bring new life and enthusiasm when given back to the larger group.

New values and very likely new and better ways to communicate will be discovered by the couple or clique when they become truly a part of the group to which they belong. This should be pointed out in private discussion with the group leader and the problem minority.

Very often the personal needs of the problem minority (which are being met to some degree by their overdependence upon one another) can be met by the larger group through careful program planning.

THE SOLUTION IS <u>REAL</u> COMMUNICATION

It should be made clear that "communication" is far more than words that are spoken by one set of vocal chords and mechanically heard by another set of eardrums. It includes every person's need for a good self-image, recognition, affection, security, and the like; all of this is a part of a person's need to experience regularly a level of communication in which he or she, when speaking, can genuinely express what he or she feels and wants, as well as what he or she knows. This is a level of communication in which the hearer truly listens and feels neither attacked nor pressured and in which the hearer is confident that he or she will have a chance to be heard.

In all couples and in all cliques there is a certain amount of this kind of communication. Even if it is in short supply, the relationship in the small grouping is a supportive relationship. An additional factor may be present and needs to be considered. A low level of social and/or emotional maturity in many small groupings blocks the members from seeing that many of their personal, psychological, social, and spiritual needs could be met through their participation in the large group. But this will be true only if the programming of the wider group has as one of its major objectives the kind of communication described above.

The curriculum, while it certainly includes any printed material we might select or use, includes far more than that. It includes the whole physical, social, psychological, and spiritual context of the group when it is gathered. Genuine openness, friendliness, and loving concern on the part of the leadership are parts of the curriculum. A warm, friendly physical environment is a necessity. The way a group sits (in a circle rather than in rows) is a part of the planned curriculum.

The curriculum of a group is the chief weapon against harmful coupling and cliquing in the group. If a curriculum speaks to questions no one in the group is asking, members may retreat in many ways, including into their small support groupings. If the curriculum requires a level of piosity or a certain "spiritual" language for prayer and discussion, there may also be a retreat on the part of some members or visitors.

If the curriculum of a group includes a group of people who have learned to reach out and honestly welcome and receive newcomers (not just for the moment of introduction), participants will enter in and feel at home.

If a group plans for the responsibility for program participation to be spread around among the members of the group and not left in the hands of the adult or elected leaders all of the time, participation of the problem minority may be encouraged.

If the curriculum of a group is built around a personality rather than the needs of the group, there is danger that the insecure and immature who seek the refuge of their intimate grouping will continue to do so rather than have to face any confrontation with a strong personality who can be counted upon to carry the load.

A curriculum which recognizes physical limitations, such as limited attention span and the need for periodic physical activity, will achieve a balanced program of head and muscle activity. The proper use of music is important in this balance.

Of course, there are members of the couples and cliques who will not respond to any of our efforts. If we have done all we can do to reach them through well-planned, well-balanced programs, and if we have tried the personal approach with them over a Coke or a spaghetti dinner, still without success, it may well be that it must be left to someone else to "get through" to them. Perhaps they will grow up and reach a more mature level of response-ability (hyphen intended), or perhaps a teacher or professional counselor in another situation will reach them. After we have done all we can and we seem to be at wit's end, we can still keep them on our prayer list where they should have been all along, of course.

David L. Silke is the associate pastor of the First Baptist Church in Santa Barbara, California.

LEADERSHIP HELPS
picking up the pieces

Nora C. Christensen

Disaster may strike in many forms:

Half a dozen junior high youth are tackling one another near the front door of the church, and one is pushed through the glass door. The youth isn't hurt, but the door is smashed.

The youth sponsors have an interesting session planned for the evening, but it never gets off the ground because the youth giggle, tease, won't listen, won't make an effort to cooperate.

The youth minister and his wife invite the group to an overnight in the basement recreation room of their home. The youth leave messy food around, shake their pop and fizz it all over the ceiling, and otherwise create havoc in the minister's home.

Three of the girls in the group get into such a hassle on their way out after the meeting that two of them are considering not coming anymore because of personality conflicts with the third.

Do any of these situations sound like something that might happen in your youth group? These incidents actually did happen in different times and places. The question that faced the sponsors after each was (in some cases, quite literally!), "How do I pick up the pieces?"

Perhaps a clue to the answer could be found if you were to talk to the adult sponsors today. In each case, they could tell you that both they and the group learned a valuable lesson from their experience—information that was useful in future sessions with the group.

Here are several suggestions you might use to put your situation in perspective and help you decide how to begin to pick up the pieces:

1. **Face the situation;** define just how much of a disaster it is. (It is hoped that it's not as bad as it seemed at first!)

The matter of the door was rather serious and could have been even worse if the youth had been hurt. The problem of the broken door certainly required immediate attention.

The disaster with the program that failed actually wasn't even noticed by the group. They were too busy having a good time. The sponsors were the only ones frustrated and unhappy at that time; the youth didn't know they were losing out on anything.

2. **Define** the cause of the problem: What did you as a sponsor contribute to the problem? What did the youth contribute to the problem?

In the case of the broken door, the sponsor was young and inexperienced and working alone; he had more responsibility than he could handle. The youth in that situation hadn't learned to have respect for church property; they were irresponsible and out of control.

The session that never got off the ground happened because the youth didn't buy into the program and didn't relate to what the sponsors were trying to do.

The problem of the three girls happened because two of them were teasing the third. They should have known better because the third always had difficulties getting along with her peers and had never been able to cope with teasing.

3. **Decide** what to do about the problem that will make the group a better group for the future.

The young and inexperienced youth sponsor and the trustees decided together that there would always be at least one older adult working with the sponsor and that the group could not meet if this was not the case. This gave much needed support to the youth sponsor and helped the behavior of the group.

The sponsors of the group who didn't buy into the program for the evening came to two decisions: They decided to spend more time explaining to the group what was going to happen and what was expected of them in the session. They also decided to include the youth in planning and leading each session so that they would feel a sense of ownership in the program.

The youth minister and his wife cleaned up their home and the next week had a fruitful discussion with the group about respect for the property of others.

The sponsor of the three girls was able to talk with the two and encourage them to come back and not give up on the situation. Because of conflicts within the group, many sessions were planned to help the youth learn to be kind and supportive of one another.

4. Above all, **communicate.**

In each of the above situations, good communication among the people involved was necessary for resolving the problem in a way that was helpful for the group.

Let the youth know your feelings about the disaster and why you think it happened. Let them tell you their feelings, why they think it happened. Involve the group in deciding what to do about the problem. Apologies and forgiveness may be in order for lost tempers and harsh words during the fiasco. Don't hesitate to do either.

In your thinking through the disaster, it's helpful to have the insight of another person. Communicate your problem to a person you know is a good "sounding board" for you.

If necessary, communicate with parents of the youth involved, appropriate church boards, your pastor, or others who need to know about the situation.

Disasters do happen in spite of the best-laid plans. The attitude that will help most as you go about picking up the pieces is to concentrate on the question "How can this disaster be a learning experience which will be helpful to the group?" Think through the situation that caused the incident and what can be done to change the situation to help prevent it from happening again.

Don't try to carry the whole problem of the disaster on your own shoulders. Communicate the problem to the group and other helpful people. Enlist their aid or support in picking up the pieces. Then the task will feel much easier!

Nora C. Christensen is a youth worker in her church in Omaha, Nebraska, and helps with planning for youth ministry for the Nebraska Baptist churches.

ADDITIONAL RESOURCES

(all prices subject to change)

PROGRAM RESOURCES

Designs in Affective Education: A Teacher Resource Program for Junior and Senior High by Elizabeth W. Flynn and John LaFaso. A helpful collection of 126 effective teaching strategies on the general topics of communication, freedom, happiness, life, peace, and love. Each strategy includes a clearly stated purpose, background information, a description of the procedure, and related resources. These programs could be used in any learning setting with junior highs. $10 (Paulist Press)

Developing the Art of Discussion by John H. Bushman and Sandra Jones. A book that contains a series of exercises to help groups develop the skills of discussion. The material is graded from the first steps of getting acquainted to deeper levels of communication. $2.50 (Judson Press)

Dignity '76 by Kenneth Christiansen. A simulation board game for four to eight persons in which the players seek to achieve dignity as they draw cards which give them a good experience which moves them ahead or an oppressive experience which sends them back. This game would be worthwhile to use as an intergenerational activity. $6.95 (Friendship Press)

Follow Me. A film about a Christian family—father, mother, and two teenage children—who decide to take seriously Jesus' challenge to be committed disciples. In so doing, they find themselves involved in a number of very human confrontations as they go about their daily tasks. Rental—$30, available through American Baptist Films, Valley Forge, PA 19481 (Produced by Family Films)

Food for Thought: A Population Simulation Kit. A collection of activities to teach about population problems by involving learners in simulations. These simulations deal with population growth and distribution, food resources, land use, immigration, family

size, overcrowding, and environment. The kit also includes resource materials of charts, graphs, data sheets, and sample scripts that are useful. The three parts can be completed in less than an hour or can be expanded through optional activities for a longer period. Most of the activities need twenty-five to one hundred people, but some can be adapted for a smaller number. These simulations can be used with junior highs or in an intergenerational setting. $3 (Population Institute, 110 Maryland Ave. NE, Washington, DC 20002)

A Fuzzy Tale. An excellent animated parable about a family who freely gave out warm fuzzies until a con man convinced them that there was a shortage. The warm fuzzies (displays of love) were then kept by each one, and plastic fuzzies were substituted. Love wins out after all, and the family learns at the end that the more fuzzies that are shared, the more there are. Color, 12 minutes. Rental—$18 from Mass Media Ministries, 2116 North Charles Street, Baltimore, MD 21218

Gym Period. A tense film about a junior high boy who lacks the skill and coordination needed to succeed at the rope-climb in his gym class. The story questions the purpose of competition, success, and goal seeking. Rental—$15 from TeleKETICS, 1229 South Santee Street, Los Angeles, CA 90015

Love Is a Magic Penny: Meditations for Junior Highs by Tom Emswiler. A joyful collection of fifty-two meditations for junior highs. This book contains honest and celebrative reflections on daily living and special times. This could be a delightful book for any junior high who wants to put some aliveness to his or her faith. $2.95 (Abingdon)

The Mark of the Clown. A film in which a clown transforms a passive congregation into a worshiping community celebrating the parts of worship in new ways. The film is a good introduction to nonverbal worship and clown ministry (childlike way of relating to life and worship through feelings and symbols). Color, 15 minutes. Rental—$20 from Mass Media Ministries, 2116 North Charles Street, Baltimore, MD 21218

Minnie Remembers. An excellent, moving film about an elderly widow expressing the loneliness that has gradually taken over her life. Through recollections of Minnie's past, close relationships, it is pointed out that aging people have very real human needs, such as physical and emotional affirmation. This film would be a good discussion starter on intergenerational and family relations for junior highs. Rental—$12.50 from Mass Media Ministries, 2116 N. Charles Street, Baltimore, MD 21218

The New Disciple by Joseph and Arline Ban. A Student's Book and Leader's Guide for discipleship education for junior highs who want to join the church. These books focus on discovering and accepting God's love and forgiveness and building a life-style that includes discipline, commitment, serving others, and establishing meaningful relationships with people. Many suggestions are included for activities, projects, and research in a variety of learning methods. Student's Book—$1.50; Leader's Guide—$1.50 (Judson Press)

The New Games Book edited by Andrew Fluegelman. An introduction to a new concept in game playing with the basic rules being Play Hard, Play Fair, Nobody Hurt. The book contains games for two, twelve, two dozen, and two hundred players, and also short statements on ways to change rules, nonreferee, create community, and solve problems with play. All the games share the attitude that the way you play the game is the most important factor in whether you really win or lose. These practical ideas could give a youth group a chance to try nonaggression and self-competition, to develop trust and cooperation, and even create new games. $4.95 (Doubleday/Dolphin Books)

Reality and Identity. Two excellent curricula taken from a series called "Joy" to be used with junior high youth. The *Identity* curriculum was developed for seventh graders, dealing with adolescent problems or the world in which they are living. The *Reality* curriculum, written for eighth graders, is categorized under three headings: Reality of God in Today's World, Reality of God in My Religious Heritage, and Reality of God in My Group. Either curriculum could be used for a combined junior high group. Textbook—$3.50; Teacher's Guide—$3.50 (Winston Press)

Recycle Catalogue II: Fabulous Flea Market by Dennis C. Benson. A collection of hundreds of teaching/worship/fellowship/mission events designed by local people around the world. Also included are eleven indexes of these ideas of new ways to use familiar objects, people, and thoughts in order to help people discover the Christian message. $6.95 (Abingdon Press)

Self Incorporated. A film series presenting the emotional, physical, and social problems of junior highs. The films show that younger youth are not alone in what they are experiencing and tells them that there are ways to deal with their problems. The best of these open-ended dramatizations include: "Different Folks," dealing with the ambiguity of appropriate male-female roles; "Down and Back," presenting feelings of anxiety about interacting with persons of the other sex; "Trying Times," aiming to show self-enhancing decisions in the face of peer pressure; "What's Wrong with Jonathan?" recognizing the daily pressures of junior high life; "Changes," helping to cope with the emotions and social situations related to physiological changes; "Double Trouble," showing a family's response to the mother's illness; "Family Matters," dealing with the hostility of divorced parents; "Who Wins?" exploring competition and moral decision making. Rental—$25 for each from the Agency for Instructional Television, Box A, Bloomington, IN 47401

Sexually Speaking: Who Am I? by Anne Blanchard. For a junior high class, this series of experiences covers everything from the physiology of reproduction to values clarification. Available with course design guide by William Paterson. $3.95 (Graded Press, United Methodist)

Take the High Road. The junior high curriculum of the Concordia Sex Education Series. The teaching resources include books and sound filmstrips which deal with sexuality concerns from a traditional Christian perspective (Concordia)

Testament Tales. A series of six filmstrips dealing with four parables and two gospel events. For example, *The Two Sons* is Jesus' story of two sons who responded in opposite ways to their father's request for help in the vineyard. At its core, it is a parable about vocation—God's ongoing call to be everything we can be. The other five filmstrips are: *The Cure of the Crippled Man, The Greatest Dinner Party, Gifts and Talents, Pentecost,* and *Phoney Baloney*. Complete set—$93.95 with record, $102.95 with cassette. Individual filmstrips—$17.95 with record, $19.50 with cassette (TeleKETICS, 1229 South Santee Street, Los Angeles, CA 90015)

Values by Colin Proudman. A simulation board game for at least three to six persons in which players explore issues, problems, conflicts, priorities in order to determine what is important to them and why. This game could be used as an intergenerational activity. $5.95 (Friendship Press)

You See, I've Had a Life. An excellent film which traces the dying of a thirteen-year-old boy with leukemia. Includes interviews with parents, doctors, a teacher, and the boy himself, as it depicts his life up through his last trip to the hospital. It does a good job of bringing out the feelings of those involved without being melodramatic. Black and white, 32 minutes. Rental—$34 from The Eccentric Circle, P.O. Box 4085, Greenwich, CT 06830

LEADER RESOURCES

Creative Youth Leadership by Jan Corbett. An exciting guidebook on leadership for adults who work with youth. The book begins by giving simple, basic information for inexperienced youth leaders and goes on to give added suggestions for leaders who have mastered the basics, feel comfortable with their group, and are ready to become even more creative with their leadership. Information is included concerning teaching skills, planning, understanding youth, understanding groups, resources, settings, and common leadership problems. $3.95 (Judson Press)

The Exuberant Years: A Guide for Junior High Leaders by Ginny Holderness. A book of basics about the how and what of programming for ministry with junior high youth. The book is divided into three sections: preparation, structures, and methods; also included are mini-courses on a variety of themes. It's especially helpful for beginning teachers or advisers. $3.95 (John Knox Press).

Gadgets, Gimmicks and Grace by Ed McNulty. A helpful book on multimedia in the church. It contains many practical suggestions and examples of the possibilities that exist in the use of multimedia. If you have been intrigued by the concept but wondered what it all meant, this is a book which will help you put it all together. $3.50 (Abbey Press)

Our Chemical Culture. A helpful book which contains information on drugs of all kinds, from hallucinogens to tobacco. Good for both general reading and reference. Available from Stash Press, 118 South Bedford Street, Madison, WI 53703.

Shaping the Church's Ministry with Youth (revised edition) by David Evans. The intention of this book is to encourage churches to take a new and fresh look at their ministry with youth and youth's involvement in the church's ministry. The chapters focus on questions about the church and its mission as they relate specifically to youth and conclude with several questions for the reader's consideration. These chapters would make good study units for adults and youth who are willing to work for a more creative ministry with youth. $2.95 (Judson Press)

Straight Talk About Death with Young People by Richard G. Watts. A helpful resource in which the author answers questions in the areas of grief, guilt, responding to the death of relatives and friends, and relating to those who have lost loved ones. Could be used as part of a study of death and dying which included other resources or resource persons from the community. Also, helpful personal reading for someone seeking to understand death and his/her reaction to it. $2.95 (Westminster Press)

Young Girls: A Portrait of Adolescence by Gisela Konopka. A book based on extensive interviews with over one thousand adolescent girls. The material is organized around themes which were of central concern to the girls: life goals, sexuality, adults, friends, loneliness, drugs and alcohol, school, youth organizations, and social-political concerns. If you want to understand better the girls with whom you work and be able to see how they fit into the total picture of today's youth, this book will be helpful. $2.95 (Prentice-Hall)

INDEX